Babbling on in Babylon

Of Rhyme and Reason: Volume 2

Babbling on in Babylon:

Quest for the Eleven Demand-ments!

Poetic Polemic Publishers
P.O. Box 5948
Portland, OR 97228

This book is distributed in new houses, old houses, random houses, and ransacked houses.

Many thanks to all of those at Poetic Polemic Publishers who contributed to the production of this book including:

Jennifer Holland (Editor)
Sucram Dragsyl (Cover Art and Design)
Erica Mitchell (proof reader)
Adrienne Fritz (website design and marketing)

ISBN: 978-0-578-01739-6

This book is made in America.

Disclaimer: No poets, editors, or proof readers were tortured in the creation of this book and no poetry enhancing drugs were used.

This book is deadicated to grammar and gramper. May they rest in piece.

"These economic royalists complain that we seek to over-throw the institutions of America. What they really complain of is that we seek to take away their power. Our allegiance to American institutions requires the overthrow of this kind of power. In vain they seek to hide behind the Flag and the Constitution. In their blindness they forget what the Flag and the Constitution stand for."~President Franklin Delano Roosevelt at the 1936 Democratic National convention

"Every gun that is made, every warship launched, every rocket fired, signifies in the final sense a theft from those who hunger and are not fed, those who are cold and are not clothed."~President Dwight D. Eisenhower.

"When the people need us more the the symbols we adore, than we can change the world."~Gil Scott-Heron "Black History/The World" from the CD *Moving Target.*

Table of Contents and Discontents:

Surreal/Whimsical poems = Bold
Straight political poems = regular text
The Ten Demand-ments = Papyrus

2007 Poems:

Sept.

Oct.

Nov.

Dec.

2008 Poems:

Jan.

Feb.

Sept.

Oct.

Nov.

Dec.

2009 Poems

Jan.

The Eleven Demand-ments

Mark Lysgaard

Foreword & Forewarning

S ince the release of the NEW BUSH CRIMES BEST SHREDDER: *Dark Side of Buffoon & The Spectrum of Scandals* in December 2007, the hyper-acceleration of topics to write about has been non-stop. From the final year of Bush, to the campaign trails and entrails, to the election of Barack Obama, and beyond, there has been an accumulation of material that has been piling up quicker than an agri-business cattle farm.

While many poets focus on personal issues that convey revelations of the heart, interpersonal relationships, death, depression, social acceptance, spirituality, etc., I have chosen to continue writing about the world at large with poetry that satirizes the powerful, and explores the root causes of how corruption grows and evolves. Some of my favorite poets and lyricists who inspired me to write about political issues are Phil Ochs, Gil Scott-Heron, and Linton Kwesi Johnson. These three were especially influential on me during my formative years as a writer. I also try to add humor to the satire in a way that may help people release a cathartic laugh over the crimes that continue to be committed in our name.

The last part of this book is entitled *The Eleven Demand-ments*. Yes, my demand-ments "go to eleven," to paraphrase Nigel Tufnel in the movie *This is Spinal Tap*. The Eleven Demand-ments are just that—demands that the American people need to make on their government so that we as a people can live and thrive in a sustainable democracy that respects truth and justice. I hope you enjoy this new collection of poetic polemics and as Linton Kwesi Johnson says, "Poetry like medicine should be taken in small doses."

Babbling on in Babylon

Mark Lysgaard

GOP!* Goes the Weasel

(to the tune of "Pop Goes the Weasel")
9/5/07

The lever attached to the musical box
Turns on the axis of evil,
And tension builds from all of the lies—
GOP! goes the weasel.

From the box the spring-loaded prez
(A puppet for all who are regal)
Opens his mouth, tells perilous lies—
GOP! goes the weasel.

The childlike game gets more insane
As the press keeps winding with ease-l,
Reporting lies, but not asking what ties—
GOP! goes the weasel.

We know what'll happen, but still act surprised
That troops defend oil and diesel,
For political reasons to elect a new prez—
GOP! goes the weasel.

*Grand Old Party

Oil
9/18/07

In the fields where ancestors toiled,
And grew their crops from seeds in soil,
It makes my brain completely uncoil,
That today we have aluminum foil.

The leaders of big business royal,
In skyscrapers with pet gargoyles,
Turn up the heat to a constant boil,
Their business needs cheap crude oil.

But changes in the world may spoil
Rich lands sitting on petro-oil;
Tribes are fighting for land embroiled;
Religions and wealth enrich the soil.

The leaders lead those who are loyal
For the Saudi families and other royals,
Who will use weapons to protect their oil,
The sun heats the earth to a constant broil.

Fighting Fire with Firewood
9/24/07

Are the Dummycrats in control of the House?
Are they fighting the Republo-fires?
Are the Dems fighting
The heat that's inciting,
The fear that grows higher and higher?

Eighty-four bills are on fire in the House;
Eighty-four bills getting hotter.
But Nancy Pelosi
Won't look closely—
Fighting fire takes a whole lot of water.

Eighty-four bills like the child health insurance;
Sit like a roast under Repub-filibusters.
But the Dems don't move;
They've got gum under shoes.
They sit silent with all they can muster.

The Republo-busters before '06
Threatened the nuclear option.
Was that a threat,
Or did we forget
That these bills need adoption?

"It's OK," Pelosi will say,
"We control for the House's good."
But the fire spreads
And no cloture is met.
Why fight fire with firewood?

The Quick Stand
9/30/07

From Pakistan to Afghanistan,
The standards are lower indeed.
Dick Cheney smirks standing knee-deep
In a sea of blood money and greed.

We have Kurdistan and Standard Oil,
And outstanding debts at home.
We see Standard and Poors, and the poor who stand
In soup kitchens that stand alone.

We watch grandstanding for photo-ops
Like Custer's famous last stand.
We have Standard porcelain urinals,
And a president who pretends to command.

We stand down when things go wrong,
Do handstands when we're not sure.
United we fall, and divided we stand,
And quickstands on desert floors.

Mark Lysgaard

Street Corner Currency
10/01/07

Currently the currency
That measures weights and dollars,
Stands on a corner with a sign:
"Will Work for Wealth or Squalor!"

George Washington stands battered, torn;
Holding a sign that he needs aid.
His paper-thin face—ripped by the Feds
Has seen much better days.

He stands next to lowly Peso,
Who is curled up on the ground,
A bottle of booze between them—
World markets drive them down.

A hedge-fund-hog slows down for George,
And pretends to pick him up,
Then guns the car through a puddle,
Splashing mud in the currency cup.

The Federal Reserve that kicked out George
Has him depressed on this street corner,
While gold and commodities drive on by;
They sell better across other borders.

So the sign that Washington holds
And those of us who hold him in hand,
Does not bode well as inflation rises,
And we're all on new corners to stand.

The Suits
10/02/07
*(The ACLU filed suits against the Federal government, alleging
illegal domestic spying without warrants. The government argues
that the evidence is so sensitive, it cannot even be shown to the
plaintiffs. In other countries, this is called a "kangaroo court"
when defendants cannot see what the evidence is against them.)*

We choose Armani and Gucci,
And other designer suits.
We wear off-the-rack and on the floor,
And some we wear with boots.

The suits that now are pressed
Are found in federal court.
They're filed by civil clerks—
The ones who need to sort.

The suits in law we talk about
Are worn by the Feds unseen.
They're suits against domestic spying
Where the public is dry-cleaned.

The Justice Department insists the suits
Stay hidden from all of us,
(Except for those who are indicted
In the Department of Just-Us).

So as the suit is fabricated,
And secrecy is spun in the press,
Will the judges see through the Feds,
Or keep the people undressed?

Black Sewer Water
10/3/07

A polluted river continues to flow
From the contracts in Iraq.
Like backed-up toilets in a million homes,
Blackwater sits intact.

Blackwater is the sewer water
And it overflows in the bowl.
It covers the Iraqi bathroom floors
With death and money it stole.

Condi Rice and the State Department
Refuse to call the plumber.
Bacteria grows on our tax dollars
As the lies get even dumber.

The State Department says to Iraq,
"We're protecting you from al Sadr!
We have a tiny plumbing glitch;
Don't throw the baby out with Blackwater!"

The sewer water continues to flow
Into desperate Iraqi streets.
No purple fingers raise white flags—
Because millions are refugees.

But Erik Prince sits on the pot,
Defending death and fortune.
"I'm a Christian minding my Navy Seals!"
But who would Jesus be torchin'?

What Does The Enemy Look Like?
10/7/07

What does the enemy look like?
What color's his uniform?
Why does the enemy hate us?
Why is hatred born?

Does he wear an "E" on his back?
Does he smell like a foreigner?
Why do I feel like a spectator,
Watching a body of coroners?

Where does the enemy live?
Which house is friend or foe?
Is that road safe to travel?
Will Hummers be safe to go?

Why are we like mice in a maze
Looking for truth like cheese?
What does the enemy look like?
Don't look in the mirror, please.

Do the Math
10/18/07

Thirteen Republicans and two Dems
Hate ten million kids.
Fifteen chumps take our taxes
And shut the Medicare lid.

Fifteen freeloaders on our tax dollars
Would rather pay billions for war.
Thirty-eight hundred soldiers are gone
In battles on foreign shores.

Thirty-five billion for seven years
Pays for three months in Iraq.
These fifteen traitors to our most innocent
Are stabbing our kids in the back.

So while these fifteen spongers receive
Their healthcare paid by our dime,
Let's send the fifteen chumps to Iraq
For their trillion-dollar, war-paid crime.

The Raver
(a Halloween homage to Edgar Allan Poe)
10/31/07

Once upon a midnight dreary,
I sat recluse, but ever leery
Of cable channels of fear, chaos, and gore.
Feeling all the nervous tension—frozen—yet
I could not mention
That one day no more dissension
Creep behind yon Federal door.

The TV cut like an incision,
Filling me with indecision
For what channel should I choose for sure?
Wall Street stocks were bursting,
Ann Coulter kept on cursing,
There seem'd no comfort worth disbursing,
Paralyzed by torture.

When I tried to find more stations,
Somehow rouse my fascination,
I heard strange tapping at the Federal door.
"Who on earth calls at this hour;
Three a.m.!" I bent to cower.
From cold embers felt no power,
Ceaseless sweat covered every pore.

But the tapping kept a-growing,
Mesmerizing, ever-knowing
In the past I'd heard this knock before.
And like a chill swept window breeze,
My nerves again began to freeze;
I begged the moment, "Pass by, please!"
From the thing that blew in fear like spores.

Should I stand and try to break
The dread that swept me in the wake,
And confront the monster—Heaven's sake!—
Still a-tapping at the Federal door?
But then my teeth began to chatter,
I could feel the pressure in my bladder,
"Please go away with all that clatter!"
I did implore.

But the tapping grew much louder;
I no longer was a doubter.
My stomach churned like cold clam chowder
From the night before.
I decided then to attack,
The door that kept me from the facts,
But found only just the tracks…
Two shoes upon the floor?

There were just two leather shoes,
Whose they were I had no clue;
But tempting me to pursue and explore.
I shut the door—rather quickly—
My stomach getting ever sickly,
My sweat-filled pores getting prickly:
I heard the shoes again behind the door!

"Why do you taunt me and drive me insane?
What is the purpose of this game?
What is it that you hope to gain?" I roared.
I ope'd the door and saw the legs,
And the tapping feet of Larry Craig?
I asked him to stop, I pleaded and begged.
But he said, "I am The Raver EVERMORE!"

Recall Nord
10/31/07

There's a figurehead on a bobble doll
In the Consumer Product Safety Commission.
She bobs her head, but will not fall;
Her agency is filled with suspicion.

What's the problem with lead-filled toys
That come to America from China?
Are communist standards really that low?
But free trade has never been finer!

We're free to get that wonderful junk,
And free to donate our rights.
It's freedumb to stress the second syllable
As free jobs take cheap flights.

It's Nancy Nord's department store;
She rejects the funds she lacks.
It's Nancy Nord's incompetence—
We call her the "Nordstrom Hack."

Let's not upset our Chinese friends;
They own a trillion of our debt.
Improving our government safety agency,
Would only inflame those Reds.

Perhaps we check the bobble head's neck
To see why her standards still fall.
It looks like Nancy is "Made in China,"
So it's Nord that should be recalled.

iPod
11/2/07

The fetish of commodities
Have found a brand-new God.
For all the things of me and myself
Are heard in those iPODs.

The ear plugs in the aural theater
Bring rhythms and melodies that dance;
You can't hear boots march with guns—
iPODs have you in a "me-trance."

iPODs, like musical body snatchers,
Drown out the government pods
That open to replace our democracy
With oligarchs and demagogues.

What's needed instead are we-Pods,
So we can tune in and organize—
When we hear our rights getting trampled,
Revolution won't be a surprise.

Welcome to Shrivel-ization
11/6/07

Mukasey's approved by a floor vote—
No standards define interrogation.
Moral relativism waterboards down:
Welcome to shrivel-ization.

We once stood like a beacon of truth
And justice in this great nation.
But the United States has a rogue regime;
We have entered shrivel-ization.

Shrivelians with their shrunken heads
Make decisions by intimidation.
The military's industrial complex
Keeps bringing us shrivel-ization.

Shrivel liberties are all we own,
Like cotton shirts in a dryer nation,
The "news" will brainwash and dry-clean
Shrivel liberties in our shrivel-ization.

When will we stop these shrunken heads,
Shrink us into emaciation?
No micro-moral-cephalics in charge!
No more shrivel-ization!

Mark Lysgaard

Honoring our Veterans
11/12/07

One in four homeless people
Are veterans who live on the street.
Soldiers who served
Stand on street curbs
Hold signs in hopeless defeat.

Why are soldiers past and present
Ignored like forgotten ghosts?
Why do tax breaks
Continue to take
From those who need funds the most?

Why is there misdirected anger
From Bush, who avoided the draft?
Why cut funds
As the budget runs
And our veterans keep getting the shaft?

Shouldn't we protect the vulnerable,
The ones with PTSD?*
Should they be billed
When their blood spills
To protect the land of the free?

Post-traumatic stress disorder

As the Mill Turns
11/13/07

There's a mill that turns on an axis,
And it's run by one named Millie.
She turns and churns
As production burns
An economy that's a facsim'le.

The origin of wealth she conjures
Is elusive—shadows of her ghost.
With the fear she creates
And warheads she makes,
She's a parasite and we're the host.

Millie strives to turn out jobs
For things that can't be reused.
Doctors and morticians
And those in rendition
Spin off from her work in abuse.

Millie sits on a bank of fear
By a tax river bleeding revenue.
And as the war goes,
Our taxes flow,
We drown in debt without a clue.

Mark Lysgaard

Buying Time
11/18/07

A cabal of big investors
Is buying lots of stock,
They're buying that which passes by—
A stock that goes tick-tock.

As the seconds pass to minutes
And the minutes pass to hours,
The stock artificially inflates
For those who buy Bush power.

Surely the crimes of George BushCo
Should devaluate his stock,
And time should be running out—
Not some how staying stuck.

Perhaps there's a future market in time
Like pork bellies or crude oil.
Will buying time forgive the sale
Of our country being soiled?

We have entered the Twilight Zone
And our futures are traded now,
Why are we buying junk war bonds
When foreign companies make us bow?

Who are those buying time
For Bush crimes present and past?
Could it be Pelosi and Reid
Find their stocks are sinking fast?

The War on Thanksgiving
(from Bill O'Reilly's point of view)
11/19/07

Bill O'Reilly is rallying the troops;
The war on Thanksgiving has him whining!
Muslims and Liberals are hurling bombs
At the Coalition of the Dining!

Violent villains of the Liberal Left
(including vindictive vegetarians),
Want us to digest Tofurkey—
No tryptophan for Tryptophanians.

They want to outlaw mashed potatoes
And the gravy train O'Reilly rides.
They want to stop all those preservatives
Like tasty formaldehyde.

They have plans—like Body Snatchers—
To replace our big menu tradition.
"Once you eat those soy-based products,
You're committing acts of sedition!

"We need cranberry jelly and apple pie
And Stove Top stuffing in the bird!
But those traitorous Liberals want to outlaw
Even earmarks, I overheard."

We all must prepare, with forks and knives,
Against Liberals with devious plans.
Let's call Colonel Sanders before
We see Bill eat green eggs and ham.

Tales of Terence the Terrorist Turkey
11/20/07

A prisoner escaped from the Butterball farm,
Like a jailed Guantanamo inmate.
He never was charged,
But he did grow large,
And feared he'd land on a plate.

An APB went out on the streets,
Homeland Security was notified.
This feathered hood
Was up to no good,
And should be caught, fricasseed or fried.

Terence made his way to the city,
Incognito with a beard he would blend.
No one there would expect
A turkey suspect,
'Cept a rooster with his sexy hens.

He dropped by Tarantino's place
For guns and some ammunition.
This turkey-as-chicken
Was not finger lickin',
But dangerous in feathered suspicion.

Then he walked into a fast-food joint,
And found a man with a white goatee.
He had black-framed glasses,
Spoke slow as molasses, saying
"Howdy...I own KFC."

» » » » » »

Terence the turkey realized in a hurry
He had entered the enemy's den.
But instead of dreading
Where this was heading,
He grabbed the Colonel by his chin.

"I think I'd like some lead-filled Colonel,"
Said Terence, a feathered Scarface.
Then he grabbed the goatee
And said "Listen to me,
I want a chopper to get out of this place!"

But Blackwater cars circled KFC
With sharpshooters all dressed in black.
And then a bald man
Came out of a van
Sucking a lollipop, just like Kojak.

"Who loves ya, baby?" came the bull-horned voice,
"Who loves yams and hot pumpkin pie?"
"Not me," said Terry
"But the Colonel looks very
Like a sitting duck who wants to get fried!"

"Do what he says!" yelled Colonel Sanders,
"He's a maniac bird with no soul!"
"Shut up!" said the bird,
You're the one, so I've heard,
Is a killer for a bucket and bowl!"

》 》 》 》 》 》 》

"C'mon out, Terence," said the lollipop man,
"Let's talk about this over dinner.
I got sweet potatoes
And a two-way radio—
We'll try the Colonel, if in fact he's a sinner.

"You can't escape; you're completely surrounded,
C'mon, sweetheart, and no one gets hurt.
We'll have a trial,
For the Colonel's vile—
Poultrycide and then we'll have dessert!

"We'll even throw in some sanctuary
In the Nevo Embassy and suites.
Just come on out,
We'll have sauerkraut,
And laugh about this on the street."

So Terence the Turkey thought long and hard,
Then succumbed to the lollipop man.
The Colonel was free,
But the Embassy
Was a lot warmer then Terry's demands.

Terrence the Turkey sat snug inside
Waiting for his counsel to appear,
He then realized
In dyslexic surprise:
Nevo was the real place to fear.

Desktop Combatants
11/27/07

Crisscrossing the checkered lobby floor
Hallowed knights slide on bureau fields,
Office rooks move farther to the Right
O'er desk-mines and dirty deals.

Two-inch GIs stand at attention
On the D. O. D's* table map.
Four-star desk-jockey generals ponder
Stratego after taking a nap.

Cubicle trenches of frontline aides
Receive lobbyist ammunition.
One-way radios channel the funds
As legislation rings of sedition.

Corporate contractors in three-piece suits
Are armed with vicious intent;
Beneath their depleted uranium smiles
Are lies of ammunition sent.

The Armed Service is now the Lip Service
As war wimps make office trips—
Then sit behind desks and faraway doors
Discussing moves in *Battleship*.

They say they want to protect us
If Wall Street stocks should fall.
It's *Risk*-y business in the situation room
As contractors make House calls.

Department of Defense

Mark Lysgaard

The Little Girl Who Cried Wolfowitz
(a poem for Condoleeza Rice)
12/03/07

Wolfowitz, Wolfowitz build us a new war!
The State Department's in turmoil!
We need your help to find W. M. Ds,*
But this time under Iranian soil.

Wolfowitz, Wolfowitz build us a new war!
The Iraq thing is losing traction.
Iran is our nuclear threat now—
Corporate media is ready for action.

Wolfowitz, Wolfowitz build us a new war!
The military industrial complex needs you.
The US Treasury is like a whore on her back;
Take your time while I shop for new shoes.

Wolfowitz, Wolfowitz build us a new war!
We're diplomats like ancient Spartans.
Bring along Pearle, Negroponte, and Bolton;
They'll all need preemptive pardons.

Weapons of Mass Destruction

A New Energy Source
11/20/07

It's not the carbon-emitting fuels
Of coal and greasy oil,
Nor the radioactive waves of grain
From nuclear-waste gargoyles.

It's not the clean-emitting fuel
Of sun-based solar cells,
Nor hydrogen and water vapor
The way a rainforest smells.

It's not aunt Ethel's ethanol farm
Growing sugar cane and beets,
Nor Mary Jane's herbal garden
With her secret recipe treats.

It's not the electromagnetic power
Or gyrating centrifugal force;
It's not the carrot on a fishing line
That leads the hungry horse.

It's not the static electricity
That's found in disheveled hair;
It's not the nylon *Sheer Energy*
Gay Republicans like to wear.

It's not the energy in geothermal
Or undulating tidal waves;
It's just our founding fathers
Spinning in their graves.

If I were a White House Press Reporter
W=Dubya, M=Me
12/07/07

W. "Yes, you there in the front row...
I haven't seen you here before."
M. "I snuck in past security
Through a magical mystery door."

W. "Have you a pertinent question?
Why do you look confused?"
M. "I'm wondering why we still
Stand for your lies and abuse."

W. "Is that a rhetorical question?
I'm not required to answer—"
M. "I'm just looking for the truth."
W. "You're better off looking for cancer."

M. "Do you mean like your cancerous talk
Against the country of Iran?"
W. "Their nuculur tumors are a threat to us!"
M. "N. I. E.* says they have no plan."

W. "I just found out about that report. . .
Last week. . .or was it the week before?"
M. "Which lie should I print, Mr. Prez?"
W. "One that doesn't hit the House floor."

W. "Look, Iran is still a threat to us...
World War III may come through our roof!"
M. "Isn't the threat you're most fearful of
Is the enemy called The Truth?"

*National Intelligence Estimate

The War on Life Support
or "God Save the War"
12/17/07

War feels sick and deathly ill;
It lies bleeding in a MASH* bed.
Cash transfusions from Congress
Keep the War alive instead.

War's lying on its back and in words,
Entrenched in a cancerous coma.
Britain understood she had to leave,
And take out her melanoma.

Dr. StrangeBush wants to cure War;
Surgical strikes will make it better—
But Americans want to pull the plug;
They write millions of angry letters.

"We'll save my War," says StrangeBush,
"From a quick and horrible death.
We can't let peace interfere
And take away War's last breath.

"Our economy needs to nourish War
So it gets back on its feet.
Without a legacy to stand on,
A healthy War cannot compete."

War will forever need life support,
But must die to save our troops;
But Congress and StrangeBush are pro-life,
So they'll let war doctors regroup.

*Mobile Army Surgical Hospital

Mark Lysgaard

Brown Shirts on the March*
(Welcome to the New New Orleans)
12/20/07

The Big Easy's not over-easy;
Home Sweet Home's a distant cliché.
Bulldozers knock down public housing
As brown shirts have a parade.

This sure looks like prime real estate
For hotels and condos on high;
Silver faucets for ethnic cleansing
And white investors ready to buy.

While celebrating the ground-breaking,
Big wigs bring pepper spray to lunch,
Tasers, too, will be served à la carte,
And intimidation poured in the punch.

Riot gear will be served for dessert
With billy clubs and assault weapons;
SWAT team waiters will wait to serve,
Since customers know…shit happens.

But isn't the customer always right?
Only if they've a seat at the table.
But no one's chairing for thousands displaced—
The American Dream is a fable.

So forty-five hundred homes come down
To get ready for commercial hotels.
Two hundred thousand continue to wonder
Why their government left them in Hell.

*Thanks to Greg Palast for reporting on this.

The Magna-Carlyle
(the Carlyle Group is a global private equity investment firm based in Washington, D.C. with more than $89 billion of equity capital under management.)
12/20/07

The price of freedom and due rights
Were auctioned off to a buyer;
Sotheby's sold historic rights
To a defense contractor for hire.

The private equity Carlyle Group
Paid twenty mill for OUR right;
Private owners of a public document
Has contradictions riddled with spite.

While the Magna Carta guaranteed
Habeas corpus for our day in court,
Innocent men were rounded up—
Rendered to other nations by force.

Beyond current contradictions
Of the Republican grab for power,
A corporation still has human rights,
And people lose rights each hour.

So the Magna Carta is privately owned
By a defense contractor who defends,
Right-wing dictators in the name of freedom;
Does the document justify these ends?

Who Would Jesus Save?

*(A poem for Nataline Sarkisyan, who died 12/20/07
after getting the reverse decision for Cigna Health that she
was approved for a liver transplant.)*
12/26/07

Cigna Health's
Incredible wealth
Will announce their profits last quarter.
But denied to pay
Until too late—
A charge of murder may now be in order.

Just seventeen
A girl had a dream
Of growing old with family and friends,
But now she's gone
As Cigna spawns
A legal team to defend its rich ends.

Their Medical Review
Saw the numbers unglue—
Protests threatened their bottom line,
But the girl is dead
And corporate heads
Spit, "Sorry" in the face of the crime.

It's just another case
Where the customer base
Suffers again from the money it gave.
And Cigna Health's
Incredible wealth
Makes me wonder…
Who would Jesus have saved?

Murder on the American Express
(A contemporary take on Agatha Christie)
12/27/07

The dark suits boarded the Economy,
The *American Express* (in the red),
And like an Agatha Christie
Murder Mystery,
One passenger would wind up dead.

The suits sat back in their government seats
Of this one-time luxury train.
Bernanke and Bush
Continued to push
Their way, with utter disdain.

The passengers continued to board the train,
As did investors from very high classes.
With pet hedge funds
They pet by the ton,
They toasted with champagne glasses.

Then Lady Liberty boarded the Express
In her long Constitutional robe.
With her laws in hand,
She didn't understand;
She was a threat if the truth should explode.

The train pulled out and continued its trek
On the bleak economic exchange.
All the commuters
Of right-wing polluters
Said, "Free trade will keep us in range!"

» » » » » » »

Around the bend and through a tunnel,
While the lights extinguished on board,
Then someone screamed
That the American dream
Was just an echo from distant shores.

The train emerged at last from the dark;
Lady Liberty'd been stabbed in the back.
She hunched over dead
Her blood dripped red
And the aisle showed many foot tracks.

George bellowed, "Boys, better clean up the mess,
Use the Constitution as a rag on the journey.
And as we pass
The blue collar class,
Prop up Liberty like a *Weekend at Bernie's!*"

The American Express went fast down the mountain,
Out of control, showing bright red flares.
And the cogs came loose
From all the abuse,
The American Dream was now a nightmare.

But the train would soon come to a screeching halt
And the tracks would soon break and fall.
And the American Express
Would soon be a mess
After crashing into a big Chinese wall.

The Beltway
12/31/07

Just north of the Bible Belt
On the mid-Atlantic coast,
Four hundred thirty-five parasites
Play games as Beltway hosts.

Drinks flow for power brokers
At their three-martini lunches.
Another belt is poured again
And lobbyists spike punches.

Belts are tightened with each notch,
But the belt-holes are exposed.
Nancy Pelosi is drunk on power
Like others who're selling their souls.

The Beltway gets tighter and tighter
From the money the belters inject.
They're belching out Beltway sound bites.
The Belt hangs our collective necks.

Mark Lysgaard

The Have-mores, Have-nots, &
Half-wit Will Travel
12/31/07

Halfway between
A laugh and a scream,
The Have-mores have more cuts in taxes.
The half-wit president
Still a halfway resident
Keeps halving our rights with his axes.

A half hour east
Have-nots have the least;
Halfway houses continue to rise.
Half the Have-nots
Feel hunger rots;
Half-wit laughs at the Have-not's demise.

Not even the Have-mores
(And half the Mav-corps)
Can have a full House resolution.
No flags are half-mast
For each soldier blast;
Half-wit works in silent collusion.

So halfway between
Reality and a dream,
We sip coffee with white half-and-half.
The Half-wit will travel
For the Have-more gavel;
Makes us wonder who'll have the last laugh.

Outside of Us
1/2/08

Outside of us, we are told, lives an Other
Of deep and dark menacing deeds.
Outside of us, we have no brothers,
Just enemies who want us to bleed.

Outside of us, the Other hangs out;
We're told, "They're waiting with bombs."
Outside of us, there is no doubt;
They've never read the twenty-third psalm."

Outside of us, we are readily told
"They hate what we stand for!"
Outside of us, they decide our fate
With fear we import to our shores.

Outside of us, is an inner group
Colluding with us and the Other.
Inside of us is a Beltway loop
Of traitors that act as our brothers.

Is there an outside with inside traitors
Working on newer facades?
Let's expose these inside haters;
Those who take orders from God.

Mark Lysgaard

The Shill Game
1/10/08

The game's as old as smoke and mirrors;
The networks have it all down.
The move the pea beneath the shill
Where real issues can't be found.

Let's hear more about Hillary's tears,
Or Barack's Mid-Eastern middle name.
The pundits shill at the network tables;
Real issues are not part of the game.

I thought I saw an issue once
Under a network shill.
But Wolf, and Tim, and Bob assured me,
"No news is here to fill."

It's the Coalition of the Shilling;
With eyeballs that roll and shake.
Consumers continue to be consumed—
But first. . . a station break.

The Good-Byes and Buy-Gones
1/13/08

As we leave a buy-gone era,
Let's say, "Good-bye and good riddance!"
We've said good-bye to well-paying jobs,
Now we buy less with more pittance.

It's a buy-gone era with no buy-cycle;
Outside buyers and bidders are told;
The dollar plunges on foreign markets;
Everyone else buys Euros and gold.

Today we buy what we don't make here
Like the flag of America's past.
Old Glory's now made in China,
And our economy is half-mast.

The buy-lateral parties of Dems and Repubs
Are just labels without much meaning.
Big money buys on both upper sides,
And politicians continue deceiving.

Before the bell tolls on the stock market race
And there's a run on American banks,
The auctioneer says, "Good-bye and good riddance!"
He's the neo-con liar we thank.

Republican Fascists
(to the tune of "Camptown Races ")
1/15/08

Republican fascists sing their song,
Doo-da, doo-da
John McCain loves a war real long,
Oh! de doo-da day.
Oh! he plots all night,
And he smiles all day,
With four more fascists in the right-wing fight,
Oh! de doo-da day.

Mike Huckabee and his Bible Belt,
Doo-da, doo-da
Drops his drawers as the ice caps melt,
Oh! de doo-da day.
Oh! the globe is hot,
But his race is not,
We'll see how he does when he loses his buzz,
Oh! de doo-da day.

Giuliani and his mafia ties,
Doo-da, doo-da
Sends poll workers like wise guys,
Oh! de doo-da day.
He's running out of cash,
Time to make a dash,
He'll make you an offer that you can't refuse,
Oh! de doo-da day.

» » » » » » »

Fred Thompson is tired and big,
Doo-da, doo-da
He needs a toup or a really nice wig
Oh! de doo-da day,
To win he needs a leap,
Before he falls asleep,
He sits at the ball as his numbers fall,
Oh! de doo-da day.

Romney's mommy calls him Mitt,
Doo-da, doo-da
Romney knows he's full of shit,
Oh! de doo-da day.
He flips until he flops,
He knows not when to stop.
He's a right-winger; give him the finger
Oh! de doo-da day!

Mark Lysgaard

Carpets and Rugs
1/21/08

From carpetbaggers to carpet bombers
And flying rugs and toupees,
To the dirt that flies
And blinds our eyes,
To the greed through Election Day.

From carpet crawlers to knee burn hollers
And push polls and robo-calls,
To all the dirt
That sticks to shirts
Of candidates who will fall.

No magic carpet or rug rat market
Could possibly hide the dirt,
And no Dirt Devils
Or vacuous fellows
Could walk away with clean shirts.

No pressure washes or press quashes
Are needed when filth is like mud,
Because anything clean
Is really obscene
When winners have dirty carpets and rugs.

Bend-Over Ben Does It Again

(A poem for Ben Bernanke)
1/22/08

How do you like your economy served?
Shaken or routinely stirred?
How do you like that trickling down?
Like golden showers straight downward?

What do you think of Wall Street's panic,
Down by four hundred points?
Can "Bend-over Ben" save a sinking ship,
Passing out four hundred joints?

Will Bush continue to borrow and spend?
Will the Saudis and Chinese stay hosts?
What do we have to sell the world,
But good jobs—that we need the most?

Three million jobs have said good-bye
And *Best Buy* may be a bygone.
Eleven trillion in credit card debt,
The debt's a ticking time bomb.

How many more cuts will Bend-over make
Before dollars fill the Repub-LOW-can?
The Weimar Republic may have had it good,
But are we making a "New Deal" plan?

Mark Lysgaard

For Those of Us Who Aren't Bob Dylan
1/24/08

It doesn't take a genius like Dylan,
Or protest songs about the killin',
Or people bleedin' by the millions,
See money spent by the billions,
Watch debt risin' in the trillions,
Leaders steal like common villains,
In oil countries where they're drillin',
So Hummers can be always fillin',
The blood of innocents quickly spillin',
And media whores always shillin',
We keep takin' that blue pillin',
In ignorance, is there any free willin'?
Thoughts for those who aren't Bob Dylan.

White House for $ale

*(If I were a realtor, this is how I would
show the White House)*
1/24/08

Check your balance at the door,
For rubber rooms and rubber floors.

There're padded walls down every hall,
And refracting mirrors ten feet tall.

Note shag carpets for knee burns,
When lobbyists visit for their turn.

There are pillars made of slinky springs
And chandeliers for trapeze swings.

Air vents are airing heirs of wealth
And coiled snake cans on every shelf.

A press room for Sue Press and staff
And O. Press guards to silence laughs.

There are big bidets on every floor
And lie-down shower waterboards.

A soda fountain stands in front
And plastic roses have scented stumps.

All this can be yours next year,
If the *Price is Right* when the time draws near.

Please Impeach Me
(as sung by Engel/Bush Scandalwink
to the tune of "Please Release Me")
1/25/08

Please impeach me, let me go
For I won't serve you anymore.
To waste your dollars would be a sin;
Please impeach me, so you can start agin!

You need a leader with vi-sion
Not I, who brought you de-rision.
To keep me on the Fed's payroll
Is a crime for what I steal and what I stole.

So please impeach me, let me go;
I only serve my lust and greed.
Don't watch me waffle one more year—
Please impeach me; the Hague is what I need.

Thinkers and Thunkers
1/25/08

There are thinkers and thunkers
And drinkers and drunkards,
And those who say, "Trickle-down works!"
There are idiot savants,
And vidiots who want
To play games while wearing brown shirts.

There are cynics for Sonics
And dangerous demonics,
And wankers in the middle of the road;
There are armadillos
With armored pillows
For the political bombs that explode.

There's the Play-Pentagon
For playpen Neo-Cons
Who scream with their sabers and rattles;
No more pacifiers
For baby crook liars
Who will grow up to start more battles.

There's the lesser of two evils
Between war hawks and weasels,
And those who say, "The emperor's nude!"
There's media silence
On corporate violence
Of those who own sources of crude.

》 》 》 》 》 》 》

There's disinformation
For dat inflammation,
And Super Delegates who really decide,
And the mild-mannered
Voters get hammered,
Trust big business when business lies.

There are thinkers and thunkers
And sphincters and spelunkers
Who say, "Trickle-down really works!"
Just grab the umbrella
From the Tidy Bowl fella—
Next ride may be a flush from Brown Shirts.

Bush on Wreck-onomics 101
01/28/08

"Hello 'merica and welcome to
My class on Wreck-onomics.
I'll learn ya'll some new fuzzy math
From AC-power electronics,
But first let me pour ya a drink—
How 'bout some gin and tonic?
Ya'll know that freedom isn't free
Which may seem a little ironic.
But listen to what I have to say
I'm not just a simple moronic.
We're making progress every day.
Ya can hear the corporate harmonics.
If folks just worked two or three jobs
Low income wouldn't be so chronic.
So keep on pickin' and I'll be a-grinnin'
Like ya'll hearin' the Philharmonic.
Fuzzy math is soft and warm—
I reckon I like Wreck-onomics."

Last night I took the "R" out
2/11/08

Last night I took the "R" out
To a westauwant where we welaxed.
Fwee wange Wepublicans wunning awound
Cwabby about some waskily tax.

The R said:
This really is rather redundant
Replaying "R" words without regrets.
No recourse like the Bill of Rights
No radicals who like to rest.

I said to R:
We can go awound and awound
With wevolution in the aiw;
Wadical wepublicans who want Iwaq
Fwee with laissez faiwe.

Then R said:
Your rhythmic rant is really repulsive
and I'm ready for the "R" back in ride.

Then I said:
Do you weally want me to wun you back
home?
Then R said:
I'm ready to go where I reside.

Inside Infragard
2/11/08

The executive branch through the FBI
Has deputized big business powers.
It's created a group called Infragard
To spawn fascism each day and hour.

Infragard is the unwanted child
Of big business and the Feds.
With twenty-three thousand bastard kids,
We see how fascism's bred.

In the event of an "emergency,"
These "business cops" have clout;
If their bottom line is threatened,
They can kill, without a doubt.

No regulations and no oversight,
No charges and no courts,
No questions asked by We the People,
No justice of any sort.

Call your Congress reps right now;
Call them about Infragard!
When business has the power of the state,
We lose in all regards.

Mark Lysgaard

If John McCain Were Elmer Fudd
2/13/08

Last night I had the strangest dream
John McCain was Elmer Fudd.
Hunting for waskilly tewwerwists
With a pop gun in the mud.

"I'll twack them down in Iwaq
For a hundwed yeaws or mowa,
And then I'll twack them in Iwan;
My twacks on foweign showas.

"I know the tewwewists hate us fow
Ouw fweedom and ouw stwength,
This wadical Wepublican will wun
With weality at awms' length.

"We also need wich tax welief
So Wepublicans will twickle down.
Tax bweaks make Amewica stwong
So ouw wed shiwts can tuwn bwown.

"Evewyday its Tewwewist season
I have a wicense to shoot all twaitows
Like waskilly wabbits with WMDs
And tewwible tewwewists invadews.

"In a nutshell hewe's what I want:
Tax bweaks and an endless waw.
Kill the tewwewist for all the wich
And mowe pwisons awe what's in stowe."

Huh-uh-uh-uh-uh-uh-uh-uh-uhh!

Bogeyman for a Day
2/15/08

From boogie nights
And boogie twilights,
There are countless bogeymen overseas,
There're boogie bygones,
Boogie-woogie songs
Like those Bugle Boys of Company B.

Back in the eighties
The bogeymen of Hades
Kept the media engaged.
If not Noriega
Or Daniel Ortega,
Gorby was bogeyman for a day.

Is Osama bin Laden
Out there plottin'
Or Ahmadinejad planning some graves?
Let's throw a cross
At that evil Hamas,
Or they'll be Bogeymen for a day!

There's sneaky al Qaeda
Like pesky cicadas
Ready to swarm the terrorist stage;
And there's Hezbollah
With talons and claws,
Contenders for bogeymen for a day?

》 》 》 》 》 》 》

It could be marijuana
In those herbal saunas,
Or Liberal lesbians and gays!
Could it be single payer
Healthcare players?
They've got to be bogeymen for a day!

Or a free internet
Where the people get
Information so they can feel enraged!
Or the Constitution
With laws and solutions—
They can all be bogeymen for a day.

Don't be confused
By the media ruse
When the president can't make himself clear.
Is the REAL bogeyman
In Bush's mirror again?
He's been there for the past eight years!

These Campaigns are Bought so You'll Buy…
2/25/08

Labor pains,
No job gains,
No purchase power with the dollar.
John McCain's
Fear campaign
Fight terror when lobbyists holler.

Big G. E.
Owns N. B. C.
And Sumner Redstone owns C. B. S.
Capcities
Own A. B. C.
And Murdoch has a FOX war chest.

Toilets run
For slush funds,
On Johnny Mac's senate office floor.
Leadership PACs,
Fundraising hacks
Visit restrooms with government whores.

Lockheed Martin's
Star Wars' startin'
An extension for American defense;
Like welfare queens
On K Street of dreams—
More lobbyists in government tents.

» » » » » » »

Mark Lysgaard

Conagra
Takes Viagra
And Monsanto owns our food supply;
Frequent fliers,
Cronies and liars
Talk to owners ready to buy.

John McCain's
Gravy train
Pass over ethics like a bridge to a lie;
There are corporations
With moral violations;
These campaigns are bought so you'll buy!

What is Your Type?
3/5/08

There are type "A" types
And those who are type "B's";
There are typing types
And those who write
And scribblers trav'ling by sea.

There are stereotypes and monotypes
And those blatant typografical errors.
There are iPod types
And podcast hypes
And those who broadcast terror.

There are O-negative types
And types who try to B–positive;
There are anal types
And oral types;
Conspiracy types who are causative.

There are early morning types
And types who are night owls,
Albino types,
Some with stripes
And those who love Simon Cowell.

There are right-wing types
Who find McCain too liberal;
There're imperial types
Who think it's their right
To pollute with mindless drivel.

» » » » » » »

There are L. O. L. types and ASAP types
And ROFL-MAO*ists in the MySpace nation.
There are verbose types
Who really don't like
To live life through abbreviations.

There're "not my type" of blind-date nights
And types who say "seeing is believing."
There are gravity types
Who fall and bite
On FOX NOISE that's deceiving.

There are desktop types and handheld types;
Those who like computer laptops and lap dances.
There're rhymes and meters
In this blog theater—
Thanks for reading all of these stanzas.

*Rolling On Floor Laughing My Ass Off

Kellogg, Brown, and Root
3/13/08

In Iraq you will not find
Contractors with GI boots.
Contractor's gear is top-of-the-line
For Kellogg, Brown, and Root.

Contractors are not accountable
Like our soldiers who must salute.
Contractors are above the law:
They are Kellogg, Brown, and Root.

Shouldn't our deepest gratitude be
To our enlisted and our recruits?
Not contractors who serve dirty water,
Like Kellogg, Brown, and Root.

Why aren't soldiers on the front line
As valuable as private suits?
Not considered collateral damage
By Kellogg, Brown, and Root.

Why privatize our soldier support
By those who would steal and loot?
"War is Hell" is what they'll say,
Unless they're Kellogg, Brown, and Root.

Banker's Beg-quet
3/15/08

The limo drives past depressed corners
Where winos hold cardboard signs.
But something's strange about a free market
When the beggars are bankers who whine.

"Stop giving government handouts
To welfare mothers on crack!
Wall Street bankers need those handouts
So they can watch each other's back."

Bear Stearns stood like a beggar in a tux
As investors pulled out fast.
This banker's beg-quet banked on players
Who thought the market would last.

From a hundred sixty dollars a share
Now tanking down to thirty,
The investment bank got market-spanked
As investors left in a hurry.

But J. P. Morgan and the Feds
Stepped in with a golden net:
"Twenty-eight days to refinance,
Or be sold and left for dead."

» » » » » » »

Then Lehman Brothers announced
It needed a three-year loan.
Investors saw the Brothers' diet
Left little meat on the bones.

Bush says, "Tax cuts really work
And so does deregulation."
Then why are the Feds bailing out banks?
It's welfare for corporations.

So Bear Stearns is now investing in
The stock that goes tick-tock,
They're buying time before it runs out,
And investors clean their clock.

Mark Lysgaard

The United Stakes
3/26/08

The stakes climb high in the United States
As prophets warn of profiteers.
The Earth's been around for billions of orbits,
But how many more orbital years?

The stakes get higher as the planet gets hotter;
We need leadership with limitless vision.
Not corporate power fraught with abuse,
But a leader making healthy decisions.

The stakes sear, but the questions don't grill
On the networks that decide the discourse.
The stakes are high and almost well-done
By the power of the quarterly purse.

The planet is dying for a new diet
Of energy that's clean, not half-baked.
The earth is sick and looking for a cure,
But we keep eating unhealthy stakes.

The Arteries of the Economy
3/28/08

The arteries of the economy
Fill with junk-food bonds;
Corporate cholesterol builds
With subprime mortgage cons.

The arteries of the economy
Have plaque along inner Wall Street;
Our blood flows to foreign bodies and banks
From a heart that's too feeble and weak.

The arteries of the economy
Strain from corporate corpuscles;
Labor protections are no longer immune;
Infections attack all muscles.

The arteries of the economy
Transfuse for transnational patients;
Organs can't organize to stop the abuse
And the dollar dilates other nations.

The arteries of the economy
Continue to harden and thin.
Labor continues to be outsourced;
A new diet we need to begin.

Mark Lysgaard

Living in a P. O. Box
3/29/08

Did you know there are plenty of giants
And they live in P. O. boxes?
They are cunning legal entities—
They are crafty legal foxes.

Kellogg, Brown, and Root is known
To get a lot in government contracts,
But it says it lives in Grand Cayman
So it doesn't pay American tax.

There's Halliburton, the perverted parent,
Who also lives in a P. O. Box.
It's eight inches cubed and it's in Dubai;
Don't visit and don't bother to knock.

Like a genie in a mobile bottle
Whose magic will amaze and shock,
When it's time to pay its taxes,
The bottle is a P. O. Box.

The legal giants of American capital
Close their safes with private locks.
They don't believe in paying taxes—
Investors want a rise in stocks.

» » » » » » »

But they're taking American taxes
Without reporting their profit or gains,
Just like Exxon/ Mobile and Texaco
Who would spend more to complain.

These giants pay their policy makers
And judges who will not knock;
They wield their profits from our taxes
Because they live in a P. O. box.

As legal fictions in our midst
And "personhood" they readily mock,
Perhaps a coffin is where they belong
Not a comfy little P. O. box.

A Salute to the Big O's
on St. Patrick's Day
3/30/08

Reflecting on St. Patrick's Day
Let's remember all the Big O's,
Like Georgia O'Keefe and Eugene O'Neill
And the Conan O'Brien show.

Chris O'Donnell and Rosie O'Donnell
And the legendary Peter O'Toole;
We have Ed O'Neill and Jerry O'rbach
And Caroll O'Connor played the fool.

Commissioner O'Hara and George O'rwell
And the great folk singer Phil O'chs.
Don't forget O'scar Wilde and O'tis Redding
And O'gden Nash's rhythmic jokes.

O'live O'il and O'rlando Bloom
And O'tto Preminger's brilliant dramas,
We have O'prah Winfrey and O'detta
And the next president—O'bama!

S. M. U. is Incomplete
4/1/08

Southern Methodist University
Is somehow incomplete.
There's a building not quite finished yet,
Off a Southern Methodist street.

The building there shall house the books
Of the George W. Bush Library.
The books do not connect the dots,
Since the truth is incendiary.

There'll be books by Ayn Rand
And the Competitive Enterprise Institute.
But no books like *Bush's Crooks*,
Or *My Contractor's Prostitutes*.

But something's missing from S. M. U.
Besides begging alumni for fees.
Perhaps what's missing from S. M. U.
Is just the letter "T.

Bottom Feeders
4/2/08

On the sandy floor
Off slippery shores
Are reps for Wall Street greeters.
They say they work,
But they really lurk
Like corporate bottom feeders.

They swim in schools
With White House rules;
Others swim with intoxication.
The Great White moves
With its lobby crew
Hooking pilot fish with donations.

The bottom feeders
Are cheerleaders
As industry continues to swim
Against the flow—
For all we know,
The people keep drowning again.

The bottom feeders
Pretend to be leaders
Of the people who will bow to the rich;
And deregulation
In our nation
Makes democracy a bait and switch.

Whatever happened to the American Dollar?
4/11/08

Whatever happened to the American Dollar?
It was once a giant that only got taller;
It was the envy of a world that hollered,
A strong middle class with bright blue collars.

But then something strange began to transpire—
Trade policies passed for big business desire.
They moved their plants for cheaper hires;
The middle class shrank like deflated tires.

Jobs were shipped out overseas;
Cheap labor outsourced to the Chinese;
India and Mexico loved the treaties;
Our GNP shrank and wages squeezed.

And then war came and the occupation
Of the Middle East and parts of Asia;
Controlling lands for more invasions,
Our dollar tied to the petro-equation.

Our economy was once second to none,
Tied to the world's big market funds,
But now our debt has the U. S. plunge
Getting squeezed like a credit sponge!

Mark Lysgaard

The Polarizing P's
4/12/08

There are polymorphous and poly-perverse
Polygamists in Polish polygons.
There are polite polemicists who use politics
In pedantic political songs.

There are pollsters polluting the pliable public
Like Pollyannas who wear polyester,
And Jackson Pollock's powerful paintings
With pretty poly-perilous gestures.

There're Polly the parrot who wants a cracker,
And poltergeists with plenty of alarms.
There are paltry poultry planning to revolt
From George Orwell's *Animal Farm.*

There're poli-science and Pauley Pavilion
And Paul Lynde the comic and jester.
There're Pretty Polly Purebred the mutt
And more Pollys to be sequestered.

There're polyethylene and polysyllabic
And pools made of polyurethane.
There are plastic Pollys who didn't like Molly*
When she put the right-wingers to shame.

Molly Ivins

Crap Shoot
4/16/08

The D. O. D* has unveiled its plans
For a brand new gambling casino.
It's in the Iraq Hotel
Where Dubya sells
Grenades like maraschinos.

There're one-armed bandits of private contractors
And the Blackwater Blackjack tables.
Things look foreign
While you're tourin'
This casino with gambling fables.

Like *Return on success!* and *Stay the course!*
And, *We're gambling to keep you free!*
We need to gamble over there
So they can't gamble here;
We're making a killing for democracy.

There're Iraqi roulette with long-shot bets
And playing poker with policy makers,
Who join the Lip service
That makes us nervous,
And the pit boss calls undertakers.

It's the *Coalition to Make a Killing;*
As Wall Street wants gambling recruits.
Will recruits come back
From Hotel Iraq?
Or is coming home just a crap shoot?

Department of Defense

Mark Lysgaard

Lawyering Up
4/15/08

There's a new verb making the rounds
As we get closer to the next election.
If Barack Obama becomes president,
We may learn all the legal defections.

The verb is new, but the practice is old
Going back to the start of mankind.
Shakespeare wrote of these lucrative jobs—
Of defending the criminal mind.

The verb will reverb in court hallways
Where walls will hear what's corrupt.
The verb shall be known in legal circles
By those who need to *lawyer up*.

The Bush inner circle, like the hub of a wheel,
And the spokes that radiate out,
May need to lawyer up for their inner lawyers,
And inner judges with Bush clout.

John Yoo has already changed his name
To F. You when we learn more;
Giving Bush power over the Constitution
Should be evidence of what's in store.

The economy may then rebound again,
Putting many lawyers back to work;
Lawyering up for the Bush crime family,
And more traitors in brown shirts.

Urinalism
4/9/08

The urinalists
Like to piss
About the politics of personal destruction.
They're yellow dogs
And corporate hogs
Building fascism under construction.

The urinalists'
Bathroom list
Of distractions—just hot air and vapor—
Decide to wipe
What they don't like
With the Constitution as toilet paper.

The urinalists
Have media grist,
Smearing the Democratic contender.
The Fourth Estate
Has a corporate fate
Of tax breaks for corporate defenders.

The urinalists
Turn thoughts to piss
For right-wingers and all that matters.
Let's have a rush
To quickly flush
Urinalism before it splatters.

Mark Lysgaard

What Exactly is in a Name?
4/19/08

Jack o'Club and Gary Hart,
Neil Diamond and Sam Spade,
Called Old McDonald
And Muqtatar al Sadr,
And all-star player Dwayne Wade.

Boutros Boutros in Walla Walla;
Dick Trickle in a NASCAR race
Saw Peter Lorre's
Horror stories,
While Jimmy Hoffa left with no trace.

Colonel Sanders and Ann Landers,
Cap'n Crunch and Cosmo Kramer
Heard Kid Rock
And Mr. Spock
Voted for Fannie Lou Hamer.

Rip Torn and Jimmy Crack Corn,
Edgar Bergen the ventriloquist
Spoke to dummies
(Much like Rummy),
And a lawyer named Dick Rickulous.

Evel Knievel and "reality show" people,
Love to revel in fortune and fame,
But there are many more
Who question for sure,
What exactly is in a name?

The Dollar Coaster
4/20/08

The currency poster
Shows a coaster
For a ride that now begins.
The diagonal charts
Show the end starts
With an economy that's paper-thin.

The dollar unwinds
And turns on a dime;
The g-force of G-money is here.
The NAFTA tracks
Have rickety cracks,
And Saudi cogs that won't let us steer.

The subprime tunnels
Where dollars funnel
The remnants before the collapse,
And the NASDAQ loop
Will bend and droop
With pitfalls and plenty of traps.

There's motion sickness
From the dollar's quickness
Of rising and suddenly falling;
The engineers
Ignore the fears
And riders scream while calling:

» » » » » » »

"Sell all my shares,
The market's bare,
I'm stuck on a runaway dollar!
The rusty rail tracks
Warp with the facts
Will soon throw us into squalor!"

The coaster riders
Like paper tigers
Are investors with terminal angina.
Perhaps the collapse
Is due to the fact
That this coaster is made in China.

The I's Have It
5/1/08

There are iPods and Izods
iMACs and IBMs.
There're IOUs
And Iowa zoos,
And Ithaca rocks and gems.

There are I. T. T.'s
International thieves
And intrepid CEOs.
There're the indigent
And intransient;
Who "inherit the wind" that blows.

There're indigo
Islands that glow;
Iridescent Iceland's gleam.
There are isotopes
In uranium folks
Inside elusive submarines.

There's our idiot boss
With intelligence lost
When he stands there ignorantly smiling.
There're interventions
And moral inventions
Like John Toole's Ignatius Reilly.

》》》》》》》

Those in institutions
Invite much pollution
And insolvent industries in trouble.
There're the Illuminati's
Invisible society
And the international banking bubble.

There's incognito
In-Justice Alito
Whose rulings are indiscreet.
There're Ian Fleming
And ignorant lemmings,
And isolationists in igloos cheap.

There's indoctrination
Versus imagination
And the illustration of insight-out.
There are insane intrusions
And immoral illusions
That the *Iliad* and *Odyssey* flout.

There're Ibsen plays
And Ishmael's ways
Who informed us of a whale he spied,
And the Incredible Hulk,
And indispensable folks
Who write poems about the letter "I."

How the Rat was Hungry
5/3/08

The rat emerged from the House at Versailles
And packed its wares for the West.
A ship was leaving for new markets soon
And the rat believed it was blessed.

The rat arrived in Boston harbor
And he set up trade for cheese guilds.
East Indian Tea would go well with cheese,
A cheese factory the rat would build.

The rat assessed the market of cheese
As other cheese makers emerged.
Cheaper cheese was sold on the market
As cheese competition surged.

But then some rats cornered the market
And combine their forces in one.
They undercut smaller cheese-making rats
And squeezed out rats they shunned.

The big cheese factory grew and grew
With its maze of laws giving power.
The smaller rats were squeezed out of the market;
The bigger rats built a cheese tower.

Mark Lysgaard

The rat-run cheese market grew and grew
Till there was only one rat company.
Price fixing by this big cheese maker
Was a dirty rat monopoly.

Cheese became more expensive
And consumers could not buy.
At each quarterly meeting,
The chief rat saw the market dry.

Then one day a sole rat was left
After he ate his smaller cheese rat fleet.
And as he looked in the mirror this time,
He said, "There is one more rat I will eat!"

The Star Spangled Republicans
(to the tune of 'The Star Spangled Banner')
5/8/08

Oh save where you see
By K-Mart's early blue light,
Where so proudly we search
For low-priced Chinese tripe.

Whose fraud types gave raw deals,
Uncle Sam bent and kneeled,
O'er the ramming he took
He so gallantly plead-ed!

And the market went bare!
The stocks burst in the air!
Gave proof from the blight
That Republicans were still there.

Oh, say, do those yellow stars strangle
And hammer our economy.
O'er the land where we bleed—
And our wealth overseas!

Mark Lysgaard

An Untraditional Mother's Day
5/10/08

This Mother's Day
I sent a bouquet
To the biggest mother of them all.
In West Palm Beach
His radio speech
Goes out for right-wing calls.

He's not a she
As you may believe,
Yet a mother in untraditional ways.
He doesn't wear a dress
(At least in public, I guess)
But attacks liberals and gays.

This dumb mother
Unlike any other
Takes medication to keep him insane,
And for all his power
I will send dead flowers
Because he supports John McCain.

As he lies and shouts,
The mother doubts
That his anger keeps him castrated.
At the sound of the flush,
We hear that Rush
Is just a "mother" half-hyphenated.

Green Hagge, Parsley, and the Eternal Revenue Service
5/13/08

The ERS has an E-Z plan—
Parsley and Hagge can help you finance.
You can pay for your sins,
Before damnation begins,
And a demon won't lure you in a trance.

The televangelists have set up shop
And they're banking on your soul;
The prosperity gospel
Just can't be hostile
If it helps the duo's bankrolls.

The Eternal Revenue Service will help
Beyond earthly obligations—
On leaving this world
You will be hurled
Into dividends for God's salvation.

You can't take your savings when you leave
But you get SAVED cashing in your chips.
With stock in God,
You can spare the rod,
When Jesus comes for the apocalypse.

So buy stock in your eternal success,
Or your fate may make you nervous.
With a nod and a wink,
Get a heavenly link
To the Eternal Revenue Service.

Mark Lysgaard

Aftermath and Before English
5/22/08

Aftermath and before English
We walked past participles;
We swung from dangling modifiers,
And clung to grammatical riddles.

We swerved around adjectives and nouns,
Ad-libbing and advocating;
We admonished ads with ad homonyms—
We weren't adjudicating.

We preferred our prefixes prefabricated,
And we took the suffix for a spin.
English teachers kept insisting,
It's "the" article where we begin.

We conjugated verbs on conjugal visits,
And hummed with the homonyms.
We looked into the future tense
For a symphony of synonyms.

We saw adverbs align with "to be" verbs,
Eloquently emphasize their meaning;
The direct objects stood quite still,
Unsure which way they were leaning.

» » » » » » »

We propositioned some prepositions
Before they could modify,
But "in," "on," and "to" were judged
To be sentenced before being tried.

Memories jogged by a run-on sentence
That didn't know how to stop;
And fragments fell from semi-colons
While we saw conjunctions hop.

We saw Auntie Em serve antonyms
To all of those who were opposed,
And synonyms tasted like cinnamon
That wore different kinds of cloves.

We sat through state-sponsored elocution
And electrifying orators' orations;
We watched thespians masticate in the park,
Driving the religious Right's iration.

Onomatopoeia landed in town
With a "thud!" and then a "splash!"
Emotional words were overheard,
Like "hogwash!" and "balderdash!"

» » » » » » »

Hooligans practiced shenanigans
In colloquial backroom drawls,
And Old English met Ebonics
For a UFC tag team brawl.

We finally got to grammar's house
Where gramper was syntactfully singing,
"This is where you will be sentenced
And this is just the beginning."

It was our aftermath before English
And the etymology of words and grammar,
But before the words began to reverb,
We had that poetry slammer.

How the Hat was Hung
5/23/08

The hat was hung
Between the rungs
Of a ladder by a Latter-Day Saint,
And St. Nick's hat
Fell on the lap
Of Mrs. Claus when Nick fell faint.

The old sombrero
Worn by the Pharaoh
Was juxtaposed between two styles,
And the ancient Egyptian,
And Mexican magician
Stared into the vortex and smiled.

The black beret
In a rebellious way
Found a home on poets and radicals,
And the yarmulke
Worn on Hanukkah
Left home for a distant sabbatical.

The Muslim turban
On Keith Urban
Seemed so radically far out of place,
And the pillbox hat
On Jackie O's cat
Was regal when she scurried with grace.

>> >> >> >> >> >> >>

The cowboy hat
That fell on Matt
Dillon in a Gunsmoke show,
Watched Frank's fedora
Give the Rat Pack aura
On the crooner with that extra glow.

The French chapeau
Worn by Clouseau
Helped the inspector's Pink Panther search,
In the Pope's headdress
That was gaudy at best—
What else could you expect in church?

If all these hats
Could sing, in fact,
About the heads round which they'd clung,
We'd know for sure
About their tours
And how the hats were hung.

Cattle Pooping the Crap-aganda!
5/26/08

Mr. Bush has a lot of free time
Whenever he's off his meds,
Spending time at his Crawford ranch,
Or in Israel losing his head.

The Crawford ranch is now the HQ
Where he's got a new business plan;
He's raising bull and raising the bar
To see what the market demands.

"I gotta feelin' I could really cash in
By cattle pooping more crap-aganda;
I could be the leading exporter—
A gift-giver like good ol' Santa!

"There's plenty of methane in my bull
For gas that the world may want;
I just need to flash my pearly whites
So the crap-aganda I can flaunt.

"We cannot appease the terrorists
Or suffer from appeaser envy,
Let's fling the poop—at least two scoops—
Against our mortal enemy!

"I think I'll hire Liz Trotta,
She wants Osama and Obama killed;
She knows how to fertilize the poop
With thought seeds she can till.

» » » » » »

Mark Lysgaard

"Watch me House-train John McCain
Who's learning to launch the crap;
Once he opens his mouth like me
It's a toilet-time, right-wing rap!"

"Soon I'll be the main exporter!
My bull market will abound!
I will sell my crap-aganda
To large cities and small towns.

"I will have my mounds of bull
From acre to shining acre,
My bull will be in corporate vats
For all my bullshit takers!

"You can fool me once and it's shame on you,
Fool me…we can't get fooled again;
My bull will be the bargaining chips
For those Euros and Chinese Yen.

"Before you know it, I will corner the market,
Like Wal-Mart, for all of my bull—
If a Dem doesn't win the White House,
My meds may not be pulled!"

The Spiders' Cells
5/29/08

AT&T and K. B. R*
Have constructed a new web deal
For cell phone talkers
And cell block walkers—
It's so good, it's really a steal.

The network nets its spider web
And catches our calls like flies;
With satellite ears,
The spider hears,
And watches with multiple eyes.

There are now more bars in more places,
With razor fences and concrete walls;
More cell phone users
For cell block losers,
And armed guards for "wrong" calls.

The spiders' bars are a matrix of laws
So Feds can listen with poison intent.
They hold no hearings,
And Congress is veering
To fascism, where freedom is spent.

» » » » » » »

When you call and your Congressman stalls
And looks around for the elusive spider,
Just hang up fast,
Or the spider will cast
Its GPS for enforcement insiders.

With all the more bars in all the more places,
No bartender will serve any drinks;
But the spider listens,
When freedom's missin'
And KBR puts us all in the clink.

Kellogg, Brown, and Root

The Jacks
6/3/08

There're Jackson Brown
In New Jack town,
And the lovely Jacquelyn Onassis;
There're the Jack of Spades,
And a Jack who made
Jackrabbits jump in masses.

There're Jack B. Nimble,
And Jack B. Quick,
And Jack Nicholson who likes to be coddled;
There're Jack's racket
Of selling straitjackets,
And Jack Daniels, who's trapped in a bottle.

There're Jack Tripper,
And Jack the Ripper,
And Jack Ruby's jackknife style;
There're Jack Abramoff,
Who bends and coughs,
And Jack London's *Call of the Wild*.

There're Jack Sparrow,
Drunk playing tarot,
And jackpots for Jacks to raid;
There're one-eyed Jacks,
Who are high on crack,
And Wolfman Jack's serenades.

» » » » » » »

There are hijackers,
And low-jackers,
And those Jacks who never learn;
There're Cracker Jacks,
And a Jack on smack,
And Jackie Chan's jack-o'-lantern.

There're Jackie Collins,
And Jackie Gleason,
And Jack Benny and his side kick Rochester,
There're Little Jack Horner,
And Jack the coroner,
And Jackie Coogan, who played Uncle Fester.

There are many Jacks
Who have your back
And those special Jack Russell dogs,
And even more Jacks
In fiction and fact
That makes my memory jog.

Things Continue to Endwrong
6/11/08

From Ken Lay's golden parachute
To his coffin to the nether regions,
Energy speculators continue to think
Oil prices for "free" market reasons.

The price of a barrel of crude is now
Based upon market greed;
The dollar keeps spiraling downward
As average Americans bleed.

The Big Five say, "Let us drill ANWR!*
Let us drill to relieve hard times!"
But to get the first drop will take ten years—
Reality's usurped by the crime.

The oil pumps, like junkie needles,
Prick us into an energy coma.
The Big Five continue to feed their greed;
It grows like a melanoma.

The Big Five say:
"We don't need more refineries
To process our supply of crude,
Letting more oil on the market
Is not the Right attitude."

》 》 》 》 》 》 》

The Baghdad café is forever closed
And café standards are lower,
Twenty-seven miles per gallon of gas
Makes us the Saudi blowers.

The Big Five reply:
"We know this market needs to be fixed;
We've been fixing it everyday.
Wall Street helps us speculate
As demand supplies laws our way.

So keep on buying and consuming;
Keep squeezing the pump to keep us strong.
Just when things can't seem to get worse,
They will stay forever Endwrong."

*ANWR- Arctic National Wildlife Refuge

Ode to a Phone Booth
6/12/08

The transparent patient lay down on the couch
As the therapist sat in the chair;
The glassy-eyed patient was clearly depressed
And his loneliness filled the air.

The transparent patient spoke from four sides
From a body that used to help others,
"No one will come and talk to me,
Not sister, not father, nor brothers.

"I'm an anachronism now
Though people once used my service.
I just stand and watch people walk by;
My transparency makes them nervous.

"I was paid when people talked to me
And now they walk by in contempt.
My door was open as well as my heart;
They came to me so they could vent.

"I had a wife once, but she left me
Taking all our baby Bells.
I've been standing, shell-shocked since;
My life is spiraling to Hell!

》 》 》 》 》 》 》

"Do you think my tattoo is taboo,
Its blue bells making others afraid?
Does it look like I loiter on corners,
A drug dealer waiting to get paid?"

The therapist sat back, oblivious to the fact
That his patient's self esteem was falling.
Then came a tone on the doc's cell phone—
"Excuse me, but my wife is calling!"

Ode to George Carlin
(5/12/37 – 6/22/08)
6/25/08

The spotlight was turned off this week
And the stage was strangely bare,
The man who made us laugh and think
Had vanished into thin air.

The mike stood alone and quiet,
Where many great lines were spoken,
The reality radical got to the roots
When the fourth estate was broken.

The wired wit who explained that "shit"
And those six other "indecent" words,
Has somehow left the building
When his thoughts still had to be heard.

The iconoclast who loved to blast
A hole through contradictions,
Used his tongue like a caustic gun
To shoot down corporate fictions.

Race, religion, politics, sex—
Even high-profile liars,
All were targets for his brilliant mind,
Like Lenny Bruce and Pryor.

Beyond his acerbic satirical tongue
And his brooding and humorous gifts,
This gentle soul has new audiences;
Thanks, George…you'll be missed.

More Metaphors
6/27/08

There are cheats and sneaks,
And liars and creeps,
And rumor mongers of innuendo;
There're Swift Boat thugs,
And Republican slugs,
Leaving slime with slippery crescendos.

There are spoiled cry babies,
And elephants with rabies,
And vitriolic venomous snakes;
There are regurgitating rats,
And loud 'fraidy cats,
And open sewers that empty in lakes.

There are fear campaigns,
With Republican shame,
And the corpulent Right-wing press;
There are hypocrites,
With political fits,
Tey're all playing presidential chess.

There are predatory poachers,
And scurrying cockroaches
That creep across congressional floors;
There are sick elephants
That we call sycophants,
And a lot more metaphors.

The Price of Gaslighting*
6/28/08

If you think the price of gas
Is due to shortage and demand,
How many stations have waiting lines
Where fuel pumps bleakly stand?

The price of crude is really due
To the useless dollar bill,
And speculators who push the price
Of offshore oil to drill.

It's not enough the Feds have worked
To lease sixty million acres,
The Big Five want offshore drilling
For bigger profits and takers.

The Gaslight Campaign is filling up
When you turn on FOX "News,"
Blame Greenpeace for the rising price
That keeps consumers unglued.

"Those tree-hugging Liberals
Want to hurt us to the core,
By not allowing oil drilling
Off our corporate shores."

» » » » » » »

Will Bill Crist in Florida insist
We need derricks off the coast?
Will "hanging ten" on oil waves
Bring tourists with the most?

The price of gas is not cheap,
But look out for Gaslight buyers;
The lies refined by the corporate press
Keep driving ignorance higher.

* Gaslighting is a form of psychological abuse. It
involves an increasing frequency of systematically
withholding factual information from, and/or
providing false information to the subject, having
the gradual effect of making the victim anxious,
confused, and less able to trust his or her own
memory and perception.

Antithetical Thoughts
(In search of dialectical surrealism)
6/29/08

Last night there was a traffic jam
Across my corpus callosum;
The superhighway between hemispheres
Encountered a faulty fulcrum.

Synaptic transmissions were firing,
But mobile thoughts were crashing;
Those that came from the right side
Had detoured with ideas flashing.

I noticed the departure early on,
But could not control the flow;
The thoughts that came from the left
Slid down like ice and snow.

An avalanche of thoughts cascaded
Through the flooding from brainstorms;
Country and Rock intertwined
As judgment had forewarned.

I was seated in a Rock stadium
Watching my ideas clash;
A punk rocker in blue overalls
Sung Country fast and brash.

» » » » » » »

He sang, in fact, a strange melody
Fast-paced, with a Country twang.
I could not fit the voice and face;
When the backup singers sang.

But then the stage, lit from above,
Showed me the stage band sign.
My brain had entertained the thought
Of Marilyn Moonshine!

A Damn Slunk
7/1/08

George Tenet is long since gone,
But Michael Hayden's taken the reins,
A new catchphrase is needed now
Since "Slam Dunk" sounds insane.

George and Dick want a simple phrase
To rally us for their plans,
Test marketing different words,
Before they invade Iran.

A catchphrase that will catch fire
So George and Dick can sell
Kindling with gaslighting words,
Igniting the planet closer to Hell.

Dyslexic George in Bush-speak
Found words like a mindless drunk.
"Iran now has WMDs.
This is a damn slunk!"

What's a *damn slunk?* I hear you ask
What are its mating habits?
Screwing the truth with plenty of lies,
Multiplying like horny rabbits.

There are many damn slunks in D. C.;
They're in the beltway of this nation,
To see a damn slunk and how it works,
Just turn to any commercial station.

Mark Lysgaard

The Black Budget
7/1/08

Deep inside the G. A. O*
There's a half-a-billion–dollar hole.
It's a black hole with no oversight;
It's where gravity and silence are sold.

Congress helped to dig the hole
Which funds the Cheney vortex;
Nothing escapes this sinister spiral
For the military industrial complex.

Seymour Hirsh shined a flashlight
Exposing this sinister hole,
Where covert ops will not stop;
Subverting Iran is the goal.

Preparing the battle in Iran
Is like prodding an injured lion,
Waiting for the lion to lash out,
So we bomb for empire and Zion.

The black budget for Cheney's ops
Is in the shadow of the N. I. E.**
Americans are left in the dark,
By the military's power and greed.

*Government Accounting Office
**National Intelligence Estimate

Declaration of Corporate Dependence
7/3/08

The Preamble:

When in the course of corporate events,
Dissolving bands with the people must end,
Capital is what matters most
And with any means we defend.

We hold these markets to be self-evident
That not all profits are equal;
They are endowed through laissez-faire
To make their quarterly sequels.

We hold NAFTA, CAFTA, and WTO,
As well as other forms of free trade,
To bring free markets for corporations,
Despite labor concessions made.

We reserve the right to squeeze out life
As well as liberty and happiness;
The quaint idea that people have rights
Reeks of democratic sappiness.

The amble:

From its day of artificial birth
In the year 1886,
A corporation assumed human rights.
Its place had been fixed.

》》》》》》》

Mark Lysgaard

And then in 1978,
It learned to speak with money.
In Belotti vs. First National Bank,
Campaign bucks flowed like honey.

The rulings over the years sustained
For corporations' and their vast wealth;
FOX reporters defied BGH* omissions,
But a judge ruled against public health.

And now the Supremes have ruled in favor
Of tort reform for punitive damages.
Exxon can lessen its punitive load
Like sociopathic savages.

Verizon and AT&T are *Sprint*ing
To eliminate the Fourth Amendment,
Telcos commit search and seizure—
They're no longer civil defendants.

Corporations have declared independence
From the American rule of law.
The Constitution is just a piece of paper;
It's the people who have flaws.

Bovine Growth Hormone

The Declaration of Co-DepenDUNCE
(as read by George W. Bush)
7/4/08

"There's uh, no greater purpose,
To help 'merica with a plan,
Then gittin' co-depenDUNCE
Fer a country like Iran.

"Co-depenDUNCE is the goal
Fer that we cannot ban,
We'll carpet-bomb the Persian Gulf
Tuh bring carpets to Iran.

"Just like our founding fathers
Who fought for Uncle Sam,
We will fight Iranians
'Cuz we want to help Iran.

"It's like takin' out an engine
In a classic old sedan.
We need to change their old regime,
So freedom's in Iran.

"We will dip our purple fingers
And then we'll do handstands.
Then we'll do some big back flips
Followed by flipping off Iran.

» » » » » » »

Mark Lysgaard

"We'll help 'em fight fer freedom,
And never let 'em quit.
We will learn 'em freedom songs
To sing articulate.

"We'll build 'em a nice statue
Fer all the freedoms they endure,
We'll catapult propaganda,
Like a farmer does manure.

"It'll be their Statue of Liberty
To replace those Muslim clerics.
It'll be of the Great Decider
For all those oil derricks."

Exorcising Dollar-ocracy
(a poem about Nancy Pelosi)
7/7/08

Last night I made a big mistake;
Watching *The Exorcist* and then C-SPAN.
I had some mental indigestion
That brought nightmarish plans.

I found myself in a strange House
With a giant rotunda room,
It was dark with zombies sitting around;
It was democracy's tomb.

I wore a black shirt and white collar
And walked around quite nervous,
I only had one way to defend
Laws for the people's service.

I clutched the Constitution in my hand
Rolled up like a powerful pipe.
I was ready to defend the laws
From all the ghouls that griped.

And there she was in short brown hair
With those big brown eyes, and smiling;
I could see she was possessed
With dollars from those defiling.

》 》 》 》 》 》 》

I came up to her congressional chair
And said waving laws in her face,
"The power of Congress compels you
Drive dollar-ocracy out of this place."

But her face turned dollar green
And her head shook to erupt.
I said, "The power of Congress compels you,
Drive out all that's corrupt!"

Then her head turned on her neck
Just like that of Linda Blair.
I said, "The power of Congress compels you
To impeach the executive chair!"

And as her head spun round and round
Like a roulette game on the Strip,
She lost her head and then imploded;
I was the congressional exorcist.

An Inconvenient Fact
7/9/08

In February 2001,
Bush was tapping our phones.
The telco giants complied with him;
He wouldn't leave us alone.

Seven months before 9-11,
But that's an inconvenient fact—
Wiretapping without a warrant
Is illegal as selling crack.

Qwest said, "Wait a second…
That's illegal; we won't comply."
The CEO was then charged with
"Other issues" and was tried.

Congress gave retroactive immunity
So the evidence could not be trailed,
Bush spied on congressional Dems,
Who voted "Yes" (after being blackmailed).

Jay Rockefeller on the Intel committee
Lost his spine on this bill,
What did Bush hear on Jay's phone
So our civil liberties are killed?

What is Democratic complicity
In the telcos' covering Bush tracks?
Seven months before 9-11?
It's just an inconvenient fact!

Finding the CIA
7/9/08

There are American offiCIAls
With speCIAl powers overseas.
They speCIALze in commerCIAl interests
With American taxpayer fees.

They have critical and cruCIAl jobs,
They like to call their missions;
With Middle Eastern raCIAl tones,
They include things like rendition.

They're superpowers with superfiCIAl
Tasks that are quietly glaCIAl,
Like waterboarding those in hoods,
And giving drowning faCIAls.

Like jackals leaving offiCIAl kills
For covert commerCIAl vows,
The slope of glaCIAl laws will melt
As they leave by saying, "CIAo!"

The Cannibals of Capital
7/10/08

The cannibals of capital
Meet at the Waldorf Hotel.
The cannibals of capital
Discuss the market to sell.

The cannibals of capital
Eat their young at birth.
The cannibals of capital
Gorge to come in first.

The cannibals of capital
Plant their investment seeds.
The cannibals of capital
Water plants so labor bleeds.

The cannibals of capital
Eat until they purge.
The cannibals of capital
Then take over with a merge.

The cannibals of capital
Are Dr. Jekyll and Mr. Hyde.
The cannibals of capital say,
"Let the free market decide!"

» » » » » » »

The cannibals of capital
Hate government regulations.
The cannibals of capital
Demand profits over population.

The cannibals of capital
Are like cancer to our health.
The cannibals of capital
Will one day eat themselves.

Freddie and Fannie
7/12/08

Freddie Mac and Fannie Mae
May soon be on the street.
Thrown out by those investors
Who saw their stocks deplete.

But it wasn't always like this
For Freddie Mac and Fannie Mae.
They once were housed by all of us,
Till private money got in the way.

Our House was sold long ago
By landlords to the highest bidder.
The rules were changed to privatize
So our common wealth was littered.

Now Freddie Mac and Fannie Mae
May get notice of eviction.
The market falls from bad loan risks;
Lenders won't see convictions.

But Uncle Sam (that's you and me)
Will gladly bail them out.
Corporate welfare is on its way;
Shareholders have no doubt.

Mark Lysgaard

Spin the Missile
7/14/08

There's a game played by our leaders
When they sit in their war room;
It's not Defense,
They're up against,
But a game that spells out doom.

It's not *Risk* or *Battleship*,
And it's certainly isn't *Chess*.
It's not even *Twister*,
Or knee burn blisters,
But arms race to spin and guess.

It's kind of like *Spin the Bottle*
Only this time, a missile is spinning,
And on the world map,
Iran appears trapped
With magnetic war wimps grinning.

What's wrong with carpet bombing?
Iran needs new carpets and rugs.
At the Iranian whistle,
We'll spin the missile
Because greed is the ultimate drug!

GM has a BM
7/17/08

Nine months ago, GM drove their stock,
It traded at forty dollars a share.
Now the automaker
Calls the undertaker,
For a stock of ten dollars to bear.

"The market is not responding well
To our behemoth SUVs.
We're not sure why
People won't buy;
We're not selling a social disease.

"We build efficient plug-in hybrids,
But that's for the market in Brazil.
We're doing well,
That market sells;
But here our sales are still.

"You think we should raise café standards
And offend the oil execs on our board?
Don't you understand,
We have a credit plan
To sell Americans what they can't afford?

» » » » » » »

"We thought we were good Republicans
Who had a fix on the marketplace.
But it just so happens,
We may be crappin'—
To the bottom, without a trace.

"We're trading now at ten dollars a share;
Why won't our customers spend?
We just don't know
Why our stock won't grow.
Guess it's time to have another BM."

Who Really Sent the Anthrax?
(A look at the origin of the military grade anthrax bentonite sent to Sen. Tom Daschle and Sen. Patrick Leahy in 2001 prior to their vote on the Patriot Act)
8/3/08

Brian Ross and ABC
Said they had *four well-placed sources,*
Of bentonite from the anthrax scare
From Saddam Hussein's dark forces.

The problem here, it's been debunked;
It did not come from Iraq,
But Fort Detrick's own Army lab
Hid the disturbing facts.

Who were these *four well-placed sources*
That told this igniting lie?
Who lit the fuse to go to war
So Americans and Iraqis die?

Bruce Ivins is now very quiet;
After "killing himself" for his silence.
Was he the one in the D. O. D.
That sent the anthrax violence?

Are there greater implications
When whistle blowers no longer blow?
What is the truth about internal attacks
When government blames our foes?

>> >> >> >> >> >>

And what of ABC and NBC
And the other media hawks,
Who broadcast their propaganda
When war rallies their stocks?

These questions will still linger
Like a breath of cold fresh facts,
While Americans still wonder,
Who really sent the anthrax?

The Big Wedgie
8/18/08

There's a big wedgie creeping up the ass
Of American political discourse.
It divides the right cheek from the left
With verbal and theatrical force.

The wedge issue, like elastic undies
Has a thong of gritty sandpaper;
It will chafe and burn and cause a rash,
Like a right-wing religious caper.

"Barack Obama is pro-abortion"
Is the asinine meme in the cheeks.
Using the words of Jerome Corsi;
The right-winger's rhetoric reeks.

No sane person's PRO-abortion,
But the Right uses rhetoric to defend,
A conceived egg floating in fallopian tubes
Is a person with rights to no end.

They say, "Barack would kill a baby
After the baby leaves the mother!"
These gaslight lies are leaving the ass
For idiots who should've been smothered.

The meme continues like bad gas travels
Through the wedge issue the Righties contend,
That if a right-winger should ever get aborted
They could always be "Born Again."

Misfits
8/22/08

A bald eagle suffers from acrophobia,
A penguin is running hurdles,
A skunk sprays on pretty perfume
For a hyper-impatient turtle.

A square runs circles in the Pentagon,
A lion suffers from laryngitis,
A grizzly bear is a vegetarian,
A jelly-fish has dermatitis.

A polar bear's no longer bipolar,
A laughing hyena's depressed,
A hedgehog won't go in any caves,
The sun won't sink in the west.

A kangaroo bought tap dancing shoes
And a fat turkey wants revenge.
Tarantino plays a romantic role—
Without blood—and the cast of *Friends*.

A Manchurian candidate runs for prez,
Unsure how many houses he owns;
The Brooklyn Bridge looks for a buyer.
We're in the Misfit's *Twilight Zone*.

Jesus
8/28/08

Jesus holds a cardboard sign,
After Jesus lost his job.
Jesus smells of alcohol—
He sits and quietly sobs.

Jesus is a Chinese girl
Working in a sweatshop.
Jesus sews Korean clothes;
His wages, like rain, drop.

Jesus lives beneath a bridge;
He fights off flu and cough.
Jesus stands in long soup lines;
Congressmen pass and scoff.

Jesus sells fruit in Mexico City;
He gives blankets in Darfur.
Jesus is post-traumatized,
Serving many Iraqi tours.

Jesus is a doctor in Kabul
And a patient in Iraq.
Jesus carries a woman at night
When UN bombers attack.

Jesus heard the air raid strikes
And the bombers soaring away.
Jesus was killed in Afghanistan
When sixty children died today.

Mark Lysgaard

The Out-of-Touchables
8/30/08

He's nowhere close to Elliot Ness,
And she's no Hillary or Geraldine,
But John McCain has a pretty nightmare
To invade the American dream.

Some say Johnny's out to lunch,
And some say he's out of clues.
Some say Johnny's got seven outhouses
With seven outhouse views.

There's nothing outstanding about his pick,
But it doesn't stop getting outrageous.
How outlandish is Sarah Palin?
Assumptions are getting contagious.

The Out-of-Touchables are on the outskirts
Of reality without any doubt.
Out of the closet come God and guns—
Out of issues in their outhouse.

Pray Away the Gay
9/8/08

There's an invisible right-wing detergent
Sold in mega-churches today.
Raise your hands
With a Godly plan
So you can pray away the gay.

You may need to speak in tongues,
If you don't know what to say.
Let Ted Haggard,
Or Jimmy Swaggart,
Help you pray away the gay.

Don't look at that manly man;
Don't let your red eyes stray.
Let Larry Craig
Help you beg
To pray away the gay.

Now exorcise those gay demons—
Like Liberace—if you pay.
Then up we'll clean
All your wet dreams
So you can pray away the gay.

》》》》》》

Mark Lysgaard

For 9.99 you'll get a shower cap
A waterproof plastic beret;
And "John 3:16"
Inscribes the meme;
So you can wash away the gay.

There is light at the end of your tunnel
Let Pastor Croom* lead the way.
And there's no failin'
When Sarah Palin
Helps you pray away the gay.

*Pastor Croom of Wasilla Bible Church in
Wasilla, AK

Tools of the Traitors
9/8/08

The cry erupts from the RNC:
"We must continue to drill!
The Earth is just an expendable tool
That Jesus and the rapture will fill!"

If the people aren't getting screwed
By tax brackets for the rich,
We're hammered by media giants,
Nailed to hinge and hitch.

The media hacksaws off the issues
Holding personalities in a vise.
The loathing lathe shears off the facts
And your rights are sacrificed.

Sandpaper sands your civil rights
And sawdust mounds will grow.
McCain and Palin use an old dustpan
To sweep underneath your nose.

The Right continues to hang the Left
As the off-balance level wavers.
These are the tools the Right likes to use—
These are the tools of the traitors.

Mark Lysgaard

The Year of the Smear
8/10/08

You may have seen some bad smears
After a rollercoaster ride,
Or the kind of smears on a NASCAR track
Where tires burn and slide.

But this year there are skid marks
Coming from a dirty campaign;
Lies and distortions are the ugly smears
We see from John McCain.

"Obama wants to teach sex ed
To little girls and boys";
But this smear is from a real pervert
The Right likes to employ.

The politics of personal destruction
Are smears like grease on glass.
Can the people see through the lies?
Will Big Media let them pass?

McPalin takes this pathology
And spreads the lies with fears.
"Barack is a friend of terrorists!"
It's been a very slippery year.

Jesus Loves You
9/15/08

Last night I had a strange dream;
I walked into a coliseum.
It was a place from the Roman past
You'd find in any museum.

But this place had a lot of people,
Sitting in stadium seats.
Centurion guards made me stand in the court,
Like a lamb waiting defeat.

And then the Messiah stood across the court
With long hair and scraggly beard;
He held a stick with a fibrous net
And things were getting weird.

A guard handed me a stick as well
With a strong and fibrous net,
And then Pilate said,
     "Defend yourself!"
The Romans placed their bets.

     "But I don't want to fight with Jesus,
     He's the messiah and I feel blessed."
Pilate roared,
     "You'd better defend yourself;
     It's a matter of life and death."

» » » » » »

Mark Lysgaard

Then Jesus threw a ball in the air
And racket met ball with a smack.
The ball traveled so heavenly fast,
I felt I was under attack.

I could not return the messiah's serve;
His ace was perfect and true.
And after the tennis match was over
The ref said,
             "Jesus—loves—you."

Burning Economies Give You So Much More...
9/18/08

The plane burns fiercely on its descent,
The captain says, "Get ready for the heat!
This is gonna be one heckuva ride—
Let's land it on Wall Street!

"We're only at ten thousand feet,
But we've dropped five hundred points."
The captain turned his sweating head
To pass financial joints.

"Please flip your portfolios to their upright position
And tighten your security belts.
You're Blackberry pie is à la mode;
And the economy makes it melt."

Then Dick Fold of Lehman Brothers,
Feeling pretty damn super,
Leaves the plane with a golden chute
Smiling like D. B. Cooper.*

Next, Chuck Prince from CitiGroup
Jumps with forty mill;
Floating softly down to Earth,
Commuters pay his bill.

» » » » » »

Jimmy Kane from Bear Stearns
Parachutes with thirty mill;
"The passengers shouldn't whine," he says
"But swallow their chill pills."

The Big Three automakers want
Golden chutes worth twenty-five bill,
More socialism for corporate losses
While innocent mugs get killed.

AIG begs on its knees
For liquid insurance it lacks;
"Here's eight-five bill, my corporate friend."
It's socialism, but on crack.

The golden chutes have left the plane,
And the economy continues to dive.
The Mount Everest debt we're about to hit
Makes you think, why didn't I drive?

*"D. B. Cooper" is the name attributed to a
man who hijacked a Boeing 727 aircraft in the
United States on November 24, 1971; he received
US$200,000 in ransom, and parachuted from the
plane.

Banks, Baths, and Beyond
9/22/08

The store of whores
Is opening its doors
And assets to the highest bidder,
And deregulators
Hate investigators
Going through records like litter.

This big chain store
Of big bank whores
Is called *Banks, Baths, and Beyond.*
Banks took a bath
With fuzzy math,
And taxpayers will soon be gone.

The bailout bill
Layered in swill
Won't include taxpayer relief,
Just corporate goons
And Bush buffoons
Steal taxes from the Treasury.

The banks will bathe
And misbehave
Just like those in the S&L scandal;
The Glass-Steagall Act*
Drowned in the facts
And the people are victims of vandals.

» » » » » » »

Beyond the bath
And nervous laughs
The government will give more showers;
But the credit line
Is still designed
To keep the criminals in power.

*The Glass-Steagall Act of 1933 introduced the
Federal Deposit Insurance Corporation and bank-
ing reforms to control speculation and separate the
commercial traditional banks from Wall Street in-
vestment banks. In 1999, the Gramm-Leach-Biley
Act repealed Glass-Steagall breaking down the
barriers between traditional banks and investment
banks. This deregulation also included code from
private insurance firms like American International
Group to insure speculative banks with "credit de-
fault swaps." A credit default swap (CDS) is a credit
derivative contract between two counterparties. The
buyer makes periodic payments to the seller, and in
return receives a payoff if an underlying financial
instrument defaults. The industry could not use the
word "insurance" or it would be subject to regula-
tion by congressional oversight and the SEC.
~ CFA Institute. (2008). Derivatives and Alterna-
tive Investments. pg G-11. Boston: Pearson Cus-
tom Publishing

Possessed by Dr. Seuss
9/30/08

I've never been to Wall Street
Or to streets of walls that grow.
I've never seen the Iron Curtain,
Or the "Curtain of Irony" close.

I've heard that walls have ears
Whenever I was given the floor.
I've never seen the glass ceiling
Because I was shown the door.

I've never been in a crowded fire
When someone yells, "THEATER!"
But I always thought we should elect
Smart and capable leaders.

And how did "fun" ever make it in "funeral?"
And why don't funeral directors say,
"Come on in and we'll let you down!"
Or "Let's talk about layaway!"

I also wonder why *The Iceman Cometh*
When he keeps *Waiting for Godot?*
I would go to a sentence hearing,
But James Joyce never shows.

》 》 》 》 》 》 》

Mark Lysgaard

I heard a whisper from a closet
 "Agoraphobics UNITE."
And then I heard a dyslexic say,
"Dyslexics will UNTIE!"

I guess I think in rhyme and meter
Because it makes me feel real loose,
Or perhaps I'm just a little possessed
By the ghost of Dr. Seuss.

Red Giants with Wobbly Legs
10/1/08

Jolly red giants are no longer jolly;
They keep wobbling like never before.
The green money trees from which they pick
Are barren from shore to shore.

American International Goliath
And Paul Bunyan Sachs,
Are now sick with fruit poisoning
And deregulation Ex-Lax.

They wobble on their giant legs
While other giants collapse.
They're top-heavy with heavyweights,
Waiting for cranes and straps.

Perhaps they seek a giant mattress
With big coils and spongy springs,
Or maybe they want a trampoline
With a bounce that a market brings.

The China Sea's liquidity
Floats loans with a nervous laugh,
But if the giants drown in the tub;
Americans who will take the bath.

The election is fast approaching
As the jolly red giants wobble,
Will the House of Reps just sit and nod?
Are we destined to see heads bobble?

Mark Lysgaard

The Nightmare Before Lipstick
10/11/08

'Twas the nightmare before lipstick
And all through the race,
Not even Tim Burton slept
With these airheads in space.

Todd on his snowmobile
And Bristol on her back,
Tundra trash swirled
About Bill Ayer's attacks.

And then in the moonlight,
Santa appeared in the sky.
"Kill that damn commie!"
Sarah was heard to reply.

Her lipstick was bright,
Her mascara was scary,
Her rouge was a ruse;
A shotgun she carried.

"I'll shoot down that Liberal
Who supports that Obama.
No universal health care!
No more Liberal drama!

» » » » » » »

"I'll cast out aspersions,
Like Alaskan mud pies,
Wear my lunatic fringe,
With my lunatic lies!"

She catapulted her mud pies
With a vigorous hate,
And the media fan sprayed
Her madcap mandate.

Now she melts like the witch
In the *Wizard of Oz* water;
Just a puddle of mascara
For a Rorschach test blotter.

Tim & Spac
10/13/08

Call me Tim
As I begin
To remember what it is I forgot.
I would ask Spac
(My brother in fact),
But he can't remember for naught.

Spac and I
Will really try
To see our ends justify our means,
But we're lost
About the cost
Of reality and how things seem.

Spac's heart attack
Was due in fact
To a hole; now he's unfulfilled,
And I felt this itch
That I should stitch
Something if we should be killed.

We're just two brothers
Unlike any others,
Just a little lost without a key.
But we hope to find
Before losing our minds
What's missing so we can just be.

» » » » » »

We are now bound
For the Lost and Found
Where we hope to recover memory,
And just like that,
We found in fact,
We were missing that last letter "e."

Mark Lysgaard

Naked Short Selling
10/15/08

The economy is now a strip club
As Wall Streeters work the poles,
But we're the ones getting stripped
From the bets Wall Streeters sold.

The Streeters parade on decaying stages
With thong rule regulations,
Goldman Sachs and Lehman Brothers
Bring thoughts of regurgitation.

The traders froth in the shadows
And raise markers as they're yelling,
Hedge funds plunge with tinier thongs;
It's just about naked short selling.

Nine million trades on hedge funds
With no delivery in five days;
Phantom stocks continue to drop
And traders want a big raise.

Seven hundred billion is thrown
To the Wall Streeters, who want more;
But banks won't loosen their lending belts—
They're not stripping for a class war.

The shadows in the strip club
Are seedy with criminal shares;
The Federal thong hangs by a thread,
But they got us by the short hairs.

The Sock Exchange
10/17/08

There are brown socks
And black socks,
White, paisley, and argyle.
There are socks to cover every foot,
And socks to make you smile.

There are green socks
And blue socks,
Cotton, wool, and nylon.
There are vintage socks from yesteryear,
And socks to keep you stylin'.

But one pair of socks
That are now in stock
Come only in fire-alarm red.
They have giant holes
That expose the toes,
Each step becomes one to dread.

The holes in the socks
Get bigger on the walk;.
Feet go through in holier spots.
With no time to darn
And no proper yarn;
We keep walking, unable to stop.

» » » » » » »

Bunions grow
On pigeon toes;
Friction turns our feet blood-red.
There are no green
Socks to be seen;
We wear credit after all we've bled.

Perhaps we can sell
Our pants to quell
The demands from our Chinese masters.
It may seem strange—
This sock exchange
Is how we trade before a disaster.

The Grand Old imPlosion
11/05/08

There's a ticking sound
That's going 'round;
It's the time bomb, G. O. P.
Do you hear the ticking
Amidst the talking?
They're walking in defeat.

Colin Powell
Bought a vowel
And it begins with the letter "O."
Scott McClellan
Unindicted felon
Says, "This is the Obama show."

CC Goldwater
(Barry's granddaughter)
Also endorsed Barack,
And John McCain's
Novocain
Helped him bear the shock.

The ticking bomb
Like a virus spawn
Infects many Republican races,
And the little bombs
Sound loud alarms
As they blow up in Republican faces.

》 》 》 》 》 》 》

Now the race has run
The G. O. P.'s stunned;
They begin their slow death walk.
And the Grim Reaper
Is working cheaper,
Buying big with each tick-tock.

On November 4th
Time ran its course
Yet the Grim Reaper waited in the muck.
Without an explosion,
Only a Grand Old imPlosion,
The Republicans just self-destruct.

The Revolution Will Not be Accessorized
10/23/08

The RNC's mercury
Rose at a feverish pitch;
Sarah's display
On the runway
Was a vacant smile and a twitch.

Ladies and gents,
Here's what they spent
To accessorize VP Palin:
One-fifty K
In just a day,
Receipts went off the railin'.

Were clothing trolls
With media goals
Trying to get Joe Plumber to mention
That Joe Sixpack,
For all he lacks,
Wear his mortgage for media attention?

Is the American dream
To be a king or a queen,
With enormous credit card debt?
How much is enough
Of Palin's stuff,
Accessorizing and hedging her bets?

Mark Lysgaard

Strait Jacket Express
10/29/08

From the East coast's Carolinas
To the California West,
A train of thought's derailed;
It's the Strait Jacket Express.

It's a relic choo-choo train
And its steam is all that's left.
The conductor smiles as the cogs come off;
It's the Strait Jacket Express.

The tracks could've been too rickety,
Maybe the spikes went too far down;
The passenger car's a little too empty;
They knew it was hell-bound.

The VP car is no longer connected;
She is traveling on future tracks.
The SJE is presently doomed;
She wants a train for all she lacks.

But the train keeps traveling in circles
Since meds are fueling its quest.
Here come the white-suited security guards
For John's Straight Jacket Express.

The Town of Sleep
11/06/08

There is a town
That's just around
The corner from consciousness deep.
It's a magical place
Of comforting space;
It's a town that I call Sleep.

I'm going to Sleep
On a train that creeps
Along descending mental terrain;
And on the trip
I'm ready to slip
Into dreams I can't explain.

When dreams begin
My head will spin
From Sleep and all it brings;
And Yawns are traded
When they're inflated
For currency known as Winks.

Winks aren't taxed
So I'll just relax
As my stream of consciousness flows,
Along the banks
Where I give thanks,
Counting sheep as the moon glows.

》 》 》 》 》 》 》

Mark Nysgaard

And after eight hours
Sleep gives me power
To feel alert, alive, and complete;
And then I take
A trip back to Wake
Because I spent good time in Sleep.

All those Joes
11/08/08

There're Joe Six-pack and Joe on smack
And then there's Joe the Plumber.
There're Joltin' Joe
DiMaggio
And the Clash's own Joe Strummer.

There're Joe McCarthy and Simple J Malarkey
And Angelina Jolie.
There's Joseph Biden
And there were Joes hidin'
From Joe Stalin's insanity.

There're Joe Pesci and Joe Scarborough
And Joe Mama with demands.
There're Joe Quimby
And Jonas Savimbi
And turncoat Joe Lieberman.

There're Joe Montana and Joe Namath
And the Virgin Mary's husband Joe.
There're Joseph Cotton
And Joes forgotten,
But now I'll have a cup of Joe!

Banksgiving
11/14/08

As we approach the holidays
With festive hopes of living,
We can all give banks today
For all of their Banksgiving.

Hanky Panky and Ben Bernanke say,
"We have a lot to be Bankful for;
We should invest in other banks
In the US and foreign shores.

"Let us prey and be Bankful for
Taxes spent on Wall Street folks."
The Treasury and the Federal Chair
Smile at this American hoax.

The duo said:
"We need another fifty billion
Or the sky will fall again."
These Chicken Littles are chicken-shit
That Congress will not lend.

"Lend-a-Ben" and "Bankful Hank"
Spread the table with a TARP;
The Troubled Asset Relief Program
Is more funding in the dark.

» » » » » » »

They're preying to spread the wealth
To Goldman Sachs and bankers.
Be bankful for their big bank rolls
And no regulatory spankers.

Let's be bankful at the table
Even if things are getting murky—
Before you know where the trimmings go,
We realize WE'RE THE TURKEYS!

Proposition Hate
11/16/08

There seems to be a big typo
In the Prop for California voters.
The proponents of Proposition 8
Dumped dollars like toilet floaters.

Big-money Utah Mormons
And the Catholic church big-money,
Sent ad campaign big dollars
Like bees attracted to honey.

Californians need help deciding
For equal protection under the law,
And love thy neighbor as thyself
Has dangerous equal rights flaws.

But does a marriage ceremony
Have anything to do with the State?
If couples have civil unions,
Then there is no marriage mandate.

Homophobes say, "We can't have 'mendate'
Or 'womendate' would disparage,
Institutions that the Bible holds
Like all those multiple marriages."

» » » » » » »

The Ku Klux Klan raises money
To outlaw mixed-marriage laws.
If the voters vote to pass this bowel,
Will the people abide the flaw?

Don't state constitutions require
Two-thirds to pass amendments?
How did this Craposition pass?
Why is democracy the defendant?

Proposition Hate must end
So all can love who they choose;
The Court must end discrimination
Or democracy is what we all lose.

The Lends Justify the Screams
11/23/08

There's a capital corner in our nation's capitol
Where the IRS meets its needs.
It's where money flows
To corporate hos;
It's a place that banks on greed.

The Big Three automakers from Detroit
Fly in on their corporate jets.
But now they stand
With cups in hand, saying
"Taxpayers, place your bets!

"We've no plan to drive our industry,
But we could sure use twenty-five bill.
And we won't resign—
That's out of line;
We're entitled, or jobs we'll kill.

"So, corporate friends and congressmen,
Lend us your ears, money, and dreams.
We're here not to praise,
But money to raise.
Because the lends justify your screams."

What Would Jesus Buy?
11/28/08

Consumers hold the key
To that which they can buy,
But they're consumed by bad news
As the economy slides.

To buy or not to buy?
That is the financial question.
Will credit markets soon free up,
Or freeze in indigestion?

Reverend Billy and the Church of Stop Shopping
Tells consumers not to consume.
"There's plenty of bullshit going round
To fill all of Satan's rooms.

"Stay away from gasoline-powered
Corduroy turtleneck sweaters.
Cast out Botox and vanity creams,
And gambling games for debtors.

"The Devil whispers in iPods
And lurks in computer PlayStations;
Cast away the evil X-box
That is made in foreign nations!"

The Twelve Days of Christmas will soon be here
And creditors will lure and sigh,
The Devil makes his Christmas pitch,
But what would Jesus buy?

Mark Lysgaard

Aggravating Agri-Biz
12/01/08

Factory plows
Cattle clouds
Encircle sulfur skies,
Manure mounds
In toxic towns
No alarms, no surprise.

Big Conagra
Takes Viagra
And inserts their C.E.Os
In government
Where money's spent
For Cargill and Monsanto.

Meanwhile…

Poor Mexicans
Are at it again;
Work in unsafe slaughter plants,
Losing limbs,
Their pain begins
Let go from circumstance.

No recourse
Under force
And no union for a safe new deal.
No time to bleed
For corporate greed,
No room for a Happy Meal.

» » » » » » »

Burger King
And Mickey's bling
Disturb foreign agri-cultures,
From Brazil,
Natives will
Slash and burn for agri-vultures.

Taco Bell
And Wendy's sell
Junk food to our younger kids,
Obesity,
Diabetes,
Health crashes with bigger skids.

Ad campaigns,
Like gravy trains
Sway ignorant parent consumers,
Jingles jangle,
Traps entangle
Seismic smiles and profit tumors.

Torte reform,
Like monsters born
Reject any punitive damages.
Judges agree,
The penalty
Not include fast-food sandwiches.

» » » » » » »

Mark Lysgaard

The monster walks
And legally talks
Through the power of the quarterly purse,
Then customers learn
It's now they're turn
To be consumed in a drive thru hearse.

Urning Your way Out of the Box
12/2/08

A friend of mine who left the Earth,
And wore such unusual socks,
Asked he not be viewed after death,
But urn his way out of the box.

He'd a diverse way of thinking;
He thought outside the box.
"Ideas should be free," he said,
Like the air, the sea, and rocks."

"I don't want to be let down,
Like a gift that's forever locked.
I don't care about layaway plans—
I want to urn my way out of the box.

"When alive we hope to rise
So our kids can observe our stock;
But when our value plummets in life,
Let's urn our way out of the box.

"We have internal rhythms that beat
Like the ticking inside a clock,
And I'd like a clay or porcelain home;
I want to urn my way out of the box.

"Land should be for the living
So farmers can grow more crops—
Not taken up by deadbeat renters;
Let's urn our way out of the box."

Mark _ysgaard

On the Auto-front
12/13/08

Like General Lee from the southerly
States of Unicn disdain,
DeMint, Corker, and Shelby have said,
"We really have no shame.

"We're here for foreign car makers
Like Toyota ard Mercedes Benz.
We give tax rebates that destroy our schools;
We hate Amer_ca to no end.

"We don't question Wall Street's motives
When seven hundred billion we lend.
We'll destroy the Union this time
So the South can rise again!"

But voting against fourteen billion bucks
To save the Big auto Three,
Is voting against those suppliers
Who help the south's economy.

So when our economy hits "E" on the tank
And you filibustered the Federal lender,
Just remember that as the North goes,
The South will never be a contender.

Iraqi Airspace
12/15/08

Last night I had a dream
That I helped an Iraqi stand.
I was the sole beneath his soul;
I stood with his small plan.

I heard the Shrub Boy speak;
He was a noxious deadly weed.
I was itching for justice today;
Not seeing the innocent bleed.

The journalist stood with anger pending,
And I could feel the sweat in me.
It was only a matter of time and space
That I would soon be free.

And as the Shrub made a comment,
Standing next to al Maliki,
The journalist grabbed me by the heel,
And hurled me at the S. O. B.

I prayed to God that I would land
On the face that launches death.
I tumbled and twirled in slow motion,
But the Shrub Boy ducked his head.

» » » » » »

Mark Lysgaard

And then my brother had his turn;
He flew like a tumbling jet,
Right into Iraqi airspace,
Hoping to hit the target.

But, alas, the target moved again—
The evasive, dirty crook—
Let's hope Obama's Justice Department
Will one day throw the book.

RICO Don't Lose that Number
12/23/08

Mike Connell won't be at work,
He somehow wound up dead—
He was a pilot and the IT guy
For Karl Rove and all he said.

Mike Connell was the guy behind
The election curtain of '04,
The Wizard of GOP built software,
So in Ohio, Bush would score.

Connell oversaw three companies
That helped flip the Buckeye votes;
He had a server full of e-mails
That Rove and Cheney wrote.

The companies that flip the votes—
Smartec, Triad, and *Dovetec*—
Were flipped for right-wing Republicans
So the election would be wrecked.

Stephen Spoonamore, true conservative,
Held ethics above dirty tricks;
Said, "Connell must come forward
About racketeering in politics."

» » » » » » »

Senate hearings would then ensue
And Mike Connell would testify,
Strangely, his plane went down
And evidence against Rove died.

It's another case of roadblocks—
Paul Wellstone knew them well;
Now that Connell's died in a crash,
Let's hope Spoonamore will tell.

Bank Us Very Much
*(to the tune 'Thank You Very Much' as heard in the
British musical 'A Christmas Carol')*
12/31/08

Bank us very much; bank us very much
That's the nicest bail out ever given to A.I.G.*
We also got a thrill,
Getting lots of bills,
For Goldman Sachs and other hacks who stole from thee.

And so to Lehman Brothers and to Bear Stearns,
Wells Fargo, Merril Lynch and P.N.C,**
We're really only here to ask,
Your grandkids to pay the tax,
So pay us or the sky will fall on thee!
Pay us 'cause we're corporate S.O.Bs***!

Spank you very much, spank you very much
That's the nicest paddle anyone's ever used on thee.
The spanking will be long,
So come on sing along,
And you can borrow from China and those rich Saudis.

And keep on borrowing from our parent England,
And Spain and France, Japan and Germany,
You really need to learn a lot
How Madoff**** bet on credit swaps,
So spank you very much for banking me!
Spank you very, very, very much!

*American International Group
** Pittsburgh National Corporation
*** Sons Of Bitches
**** Bernie Madoff is the indicted CEO of the
world's largest hedge fund ponzi scheme that stripped
investors of over $50 billion dollars.

I Always Got the Blame

(Imagine if the ghost of Herbert Hoover appeared like Jacob Marley
wrapped in chains of debts from 1932, and started to sing like the tin
man in "The Wizard of Oz" the song "If I only had a Brain.")
1/4/09

When I was president,
It was no accident
I poured the economy down the drain.
I helped the speculators
Like hungry alligators
Because I really had no shame.

I was president after Coolidge,
But don't let that Fool-yidge;
I was a conservative all the same.
And Carnegie and Mellon
Said, "Deregulation's sellin,'
But it was only a shell game.

Oh, history, who needs it?
I've been there before.
Don't go back
To ugly facts;
It's easier to be a corporate whore.

And then in twenty-nine,
I heard the people whine,
And there was a run on all the banks.
They all went belly up
'cause the system was corrupt,
And my reputation tanked.

» » » » » » »

Mark Lysgaard

So take this as a warning,
If you want to see the morning,
Invest in the middle class;
Don't be lais-sez faire,
When you're losing all your hair
Cuz you'll always lose your ass!

The Prosthetic Legacy
1/17/09

After eight years of amputations
On civil and human rights,
Dubya smiled with guillotine cuts
And more slicing into the night.

"You say, 'I coulda done better,'
But I inherited a recession."
The recession happened in March '01
And now leading to a depression.

"But I protected America
From any further terrorist attacks!"
But what about the anthrax
And early intel's warning tracks?

Fifty-six warnings up till 9/11
That included August sixth,
"Bin Laden determined to strike in America"
You ignored as the clock ticked.

You violated many amendments
To the US Constitution;
'No bid' contracts went to campaign donors,
Like political prostitution.

» » » » » » »

Mark Lysgaard

You appointed big lobbyists
To fill regulatory seats,
Lobbyists turned their backs on us
With lies they pledged to keep.

You say you want to insure a legacy
Of freedom from terrorist plans,
But you left America with a prosthesis;
A legacy that just won't stand.

The Names of Shame
1/29/09

Bernie Madoff with fifty billion.
Arlen Sphincter's clamping down,
Mitch McCon-artist paints the truth
Jim De-mint de-mentally frowns.

Chuck Grassley smokes his name.
Phil Gingry's gang green still,
John Cornyn wants corn holes
That Jon Boehner (Boner) hopes to fill.

Jon Kyl kills many dreams
As does Bunning and Coburn,
Bob Corker blows himself
John Ensign never learns.

Eric Canwhore for the party
The stimulus—he says, "No thanks!"
But millions of tax payer dollars
Went to Diane Canwhore's bank.

WhOrrin Hatch aborts the truth
And so do many others,
Baucus and Burr will filibuster,
So the facts are smothered.

These are the clowns who hang around
Like backed up legal turds,
But many more await their orders
From Rimbowl's flushing words.

The Eleven Demand-ments
(Yes, mine go to eleven)

I f you've made it this far through the book, you are either an open minded lefty-progressive with a sense of humor, or you're a neo-con masochist paying for your sins. If you think the next section of this book is about Moses coming down from Mt. Sinai with two large stone tablets, then I have some hedge fund bonds that will make you rich! If however you think this section of the book is about the demands that the American people are making to live in a sustainable and active democracy, you've come to the right or *correct* place.

As you may have figured out by now, the running theme throughout this book is identifying corruption, deregulation, unbridled greed, lies, and militarism through the strained and alienating social relations of corporatism. In the old days, corporatism was called *fascism* by Benito Mussolini, and it was embraced by such notable dictators as Francisco Franco, Augustus Pinochet, and others. The merger of the corporation and government has been getting more and more traction over the years, yet many people who recognize these traits are still unwilling to call it fascism. FDR helped to save America from going fascist with The New Deal, and all of his public works policies helped to protect workers through unions, which saw the rise of the middle class.

We are now at a pivotal point in our history where Barack Obama has an opportunity to be this generation's FDR. We must continue to put pressure on President Obama to grant the people everything from universal single-payer healthcare to progressive tax structures that make the top five percent income earners pay more for the priviliges they receive in our society. Furthermore, we must believe that there is a thing called good government where we have good and decent people in government who care more for the needs of the people, rather than the special corporate interest that pay for politicians and their campaign donations.

The following series of *Demand-ments* are just that; demands for what we as Americans deserve from our government so that we may all live and thrive in a sustainable democracy.

In solidarity,

Mark Lysgaard

The Pre-amble to the Demand-ments:
No More Corporate Personhood*

In the 1886 court case Santa Clara vs. Southern Pacific Rail Road, the Supreme Court, because of a note posted by a clerk of the Courts, mistakenly interpreted the term "corporation" as an entity having legal human rights. Even though the clerk had no legal jurisdiction to affix this note, it set judicial precedence, supposedly on behalf of "We the People."

The biggest problem "We the People" face
Are rights given to artificial beings.
These rights are just like the ones we have,
But we're real, with eyes we're seeing.

These artificial things are present;
They're legal fictions that never sleep.
They're Frankensteins on Frankensteroids,
Immobile monsters on many streets.

They were legally conceived in a court case
By a clerk who was up to no good.
They appeared as a memo attached to the page
Making legal "corporate personhood."

Since 1886 they've been legal,
Like Supermen with super rights.
With vast resources to keep them legal,
"The People" lose without a fight.

» » » » » » »

These legal fictions cannot walk,
Cannot breathe, drink water, or salute.
They're abominations for the bottom line,
Making profits even when they pollute.

Destroying these creatures won't happen,
But rolling back their power's a must.
Vertical integration and cross-pollination
Should end with Sherman's Antitrust.

*To fully appreciate the historical period and predicament we
find ourselves, please read Thom Hartmann's book's:
*Unequal Protection: The Rise of Corporate Dominance and the Theft
of Human Rights.*

First Demand-ment:
Thou Shall Regulate Big Media

From '49 to '87
The airwaves were owned by us.
The FCC regulated the air,
All for the public's trust.

Jimmy Carter was the last to sue
Using the Sherman Anti-trust Act;
Jimmy broke up AT&T
So monopolies couldn't strike back.

But then Ronald Reagan privatized,
Selling our air to the highest bidder.
No longer the air of "We the People,"
But filled with commercial litter.

The Fairness Doctrine was thrown out,
And power became concentrated.
Private companies aired their message
Unabridged and not debated.

Giant media started getting together
And consolidated power for earnings;
"Profits over people" was the phrase
As the right-wing spin kept turning.

Now it's time to demand from the Dems
That Sherman's Act be applied.
No more giant monopolies,
Or corporate stooges compelled to lie.

Second Demand-ment:
Thou Shall Reform Campaign Finance:
Overturn First National Bank of Boston
versus Bellotti.

In nineteen sevety-eight,
The Supreme Court struck down,
An election law that forbid
Corporate spending in any town.

The Supreme court in Massuchusetts
Decided corporations had a choice,
To fund their own initiatives,
Or defeat the people's voice.

Money talks became the mantra
And the First Amendment was their frame,
But a corporation cannot talk,
It should not contribute to campaigns.

Public financing of all elections
Should be a federal law.
Let's take out private money,
This is democracy's call.

Third Demand-ment
De-privatize the Vote:

The next step for Congress
Should keep integrity of our votes.
We the people need paper ballots
To verify what we wrote.

Let's insure all public elections
So that "We the People" decide,
Not the antics of private companies
In black boxes to process lies.

The precious part of how we choose
Should not be usurped by those,
Who work against Americans
For companies and their ho's.

Europe and Canada with their paper ballots
Use real eyes and hands.
The legitimacy of knowing who won
Is the freedom we demand.

Fourth Demand-ment: De-privatize the Military

At the height of World War II,
FDR heard this from Truman:
"There are war profiteers in our midst,
Profiting from the loss of humans!"

Congress convened and investigated,
Held Senate hearings on the war.
Many private company's heads
Went to prison when profits soared.

Thousands of Americans lost their lives
Because of greedy war profiteers—
Just like the war contractors today;
They're the real ones we should fear.

Only volunteer service members
Deserve full public support,
Not soldiers of fortune or greed mercenaries
Who kill from their private forts.

When an Army GI's in the trenches
And he's getting shot by attackers,
The last thing he should worry about is
His paycheck going to contractors.

Private contractors work side by side
Our enlisted soldiers in Iraq,
But mercenaries are unaccountable
Even though they receive our tax.

Twenty thousand dollars a month
May go to these soldiers of fortune,
But war is indiscriminate—
No matter who's doin' the torchin.'

The rules of engagement must be followed
As written by the reps we elect.
No free-for-all or "anything goes;"
No profits from our tax checks.

Fifth Demand-ment:
Medicare for All

Twenty-four cents on every dollar
Pay private healthcare costs,
Going to C.E.Os and stockholders;
The uninsured wander—lost.

Medicare, on the other hand,
Administered by the Feds,
Costs only three cents on the dollar—
A plan to equally spread.

Saving tax dollars for *We the People*,
With everyone readily insured,
Would spread the risk and lower taxes,
A point that's hardly heard.

When forty million don't have coverage
And they get sick or deathly ill,
Private insurers raise their rates
Squeezing the middle class with the bill.

It really just makes perfect sense
That the government insures us all,
Reducing cost for everyone;
It's a plan we must install.

Sixth Demand-ment:
Lift Caps on Social Security Net

The net's stretched out below our feet;
We walk a high tightwire.
Conservatives say the net's too worn
And won't catch us when we retire.

The net's been there since '36,
Catching those who fell—
From disability, unemployment, and death
It's been there for us as well.

But the Neo-Cons would have us think
The net's holes are like Swiss cheese.
They say it's fragile and cannot last;
It'll unravel in a fiscal breeze.

But the breeze coming from the Cons
Is hot air from a steaming pot.
They say the net should be replaced by clams
When the stock market's boiling hot.

Social Security is not an investment
Nor clams from a Wall Street feast,
Social Security is our insurance
To save us at the least.

The solution is to keep funding the net,
Mending the holes the Cons put there.
Millionaires should be fully taxed,
And billionaires pay their share.

The Seventh Demand-ment: Employee Free Choice Act

When in nineteen thirty-five,
FDR signed the Wagner Act,
Workers could unionize;
Feds had the workers' backs.

In nineteen forty-six, just after the war,
Labor was running strong;
Five million workers willing to strike,
Wouldn't take abuse for long.

The labor movement was educated
And empowered the middle class,
But an anti-union storm was brewing—
Worker's rights would't last.

The assault on labor soon ensued—
The record shows the facts.
The first major hit against workers
Was the Taft-Hartley Act.

It was the first big campaign
To curtail the rights of labor;
Unions could not strike or picket;
Companies weren't good neighbors.

Jurisdictional and wildcat strikes
And boycotts were outlawed.
Rights of workers were getting smashed;
Big business' powers were broad.

» » » » » » »

Today the Employee Free Choice Act
Gives leverage back to labor.
Workers can choose to unionize;
No fear from business neighbors.

Enacting this legislation
Is part of democracy's plan;
To build a strong middle class again
Is what Americans demand.

Eighth Demand-ment
Thou Shall Nationalize Renewable Energy
Independence:

Over the past one hundred-plus years,
We cultured our taste for oil;
Not animal, vegetable, or mineral,
But petrol, deep in the soil.

Our voracious appetite included
More unsustainable fuels:
Coal and nuclear were also tried—
Profits for short-term fools.

But now the Earth is a sickly patient
Suffering from greenhouse gases;
The warming of the world's oceans
Is ignored by unaware masses.

Profits drive for short-term gains
Every corporate quarter;
If earnings don't bring bigger stocks,
Investors leave for the border.

We must think in the long-term;
Find sustainable energy fuels.
Solar, wind, and hydro can
Be our ever-renewable tools.

» » » » » » »

These earth-friendly resources
Are abundant for the people at hand;
The wind and sun aren't commodified—
All people profit from demand.

"We the People" own our land,
And energy is a national resource;
Let's nationalize our energy needs,
So profiteers don't take it by force.

Ninth Demand-ment:
Congress Declares War

The Constitution is pretty clear
About the separation of powers;
It's up to Congress to declare war,
Not the rogue president of the hour.

This is not a monarchy,
But a nation with laws at its core;
If foreign troops land on our soil,
It's Congress who declares war.

No more secret dirty wars
To undermine foreign nations,
Or coups d'état by right-wing thugs;
That's not about liberation.

We must end our occupations
Of the Middle East and Afghanistan.
We aren't a country of warmongers;
We're Americans with peace plans.

Tenth Demand-ment:
Free Education Through College

The Founders had the right idea
Making education free in the States*,
TJ** founded the U of Virginia
So colonists could have a mandate.

The idea was to get away from
Entrenched oligarchs overseas,
And give the colonists a chance
To improve their lot with ease.

No one*** would be denied the right
To a decent and free education.
An educated and skilled work force
Could build a secure nation.

And then profiteers dug in their hooks
At different state-run schools.
Education became privatized;
People paid, or became tools.

Now state schools receive tax money
From citizens of that state;
They're asked to dig ever deeper,
Because profiteers have mandates.

» » » » » » »

How does a nation stay safe,
When they can't afford education?
An ignorant people are not secure;
Free education in our free nation.

*colonies at the time
**Thomas Jefferson
*** Jefferson believed the nation needed public schools
scattered around, for all white male citizens to receive free education.

Eleventh Demand-ment: End "Free" Trade/ Higher Tarrifs

It should be a patriot's duty
To support manufacturing's base;
To keep well-paid jobs right here,
Not in a foreign sweatshop place.

From the founding of this nation
To the eve of World War I,
Tariffs were the largest source
Of our government's income.

Then the income tax was added
Funding plans after the War,
Americans bound in community
Saw manufacturing soar.

Tariffs help protect good jobs
From outsourcing overseas,
Raising the duty of foreign products
Allows blue collars to breathe.

During the fifties Ike had it right—
Higher tariffs and corporate tax;
We're a country of proud citizens,
Not consumers of tawdry crap.

This demand is long overdue
To bring America back to the top.
Let's export these neo-cons
To Malaysia's cheap sweatshops!

S pecial thanks to all of the people who have stood up for justice and continue to tell the truth amidst the powers that try to silence them. This book is dedicated to the following progressive heros: Howard Zinn, Bernie Sanders, Dennis Kucinich, Jim Hightower, Barbara Erenreich, Gil Scott-Heron, Linton Kwesi Johnson, Chuck D, Pete Seeger, Peter DeFazio, Earl Blumenhauer, Gore Vidal, Thom Hartmann, Carl Wolfson, Amy Goodman, Michael Moore, Keith Olbermann, Rachel Maddow, Stephanie Miller, Peter B. Collins, Peter Werbe, Jon Elliot, Cindy Sheehan, Shannyn Moore, Mike Malloy, Randi Rhodes, Greg Palast, Chris Hedges, Jeremy Scahill, Brad Friedman, Katrina vanden Heuvel, John Nichols, Laura Flanders, Nicole Sandler, John Amato, Bobby Kennedy Jr., Mike Pappantonio, David Bender, Marc Maron, Sam Seder, Madeleine Begun Kane, Ed Schultz, Christopher Hayes, Markos Moulitsas, Eric Alterman, Ron Reagan, Jack Rice, Glen Greenwald, Robert Greenwald, David Sirota, David Brock, Noam Chomsky, Naomi Klein, Naomi Wolf, Ralph Nader, Jesse Jackson, Michael Rupert, David Ray Griffin, John Perkins, Manning Marable, Morris Dees, David Ray Griffin, Jim Marrs, Mike Farrell, Martin Sheen, Danny Glover, Sean Penn, Jim Wallis, Garry Trudeau, Dario Fo, Calvin Trillin, Phil Donahue, Bill Moyer, Jean and George Edwards, Carla Wallace, Dennis Bricking, the memory of Anne Braden, and all of those who have died to help others live in a better world. You have all been inspirational to me as an artist and writer to seize the moment for truth and justice.

Peace,

~Mark Lysgaard
June 2009

Mark Lysgaard

Babbling on in Babylon

www.ingramcontent.com/pod-product-compliance
Lightning Source LLC
La Vergne TN
LVHW011418080426
835512LV00005B/128